Forged Through Fire

Forged Through Fire

Developing Preparedness for the Perilous Encounter

G. R. Burns

Tactical Training Academy Publishing, LLC
Seattle, Washington

My thanks to Steve Harris for hammering my character and for his assistance
with this content.
He is a man of the Vision.

Published 2018 by
Tactical Training Academy Publishing, LLC
PO Box 1259, Lake Stevens WA, 98258
www.Training-Academy.org

Printed in the United States of America

ISBN: 9781980702948

This edition of *Forged Through Fire* contains all corrections and revisions
that have been made since the original publication

® is a registered trademark of the Tactical
Training Academy, LLC

To my son, William
That you may walk confidently into life with humility and
honor for our King

Contents

Introduction

*F*orged Through Fire: Developing Preparedness for the
Perilous Encounter* was originally compiled as a
response to many requests for further materials on
emergency preparedness. As an emergency preparedness
trainer, I've noticed that organizations preparing for or reeling
from violent, traumatic events often only take their employees
through a two- or three-hour "educational" seminar. Even
worse, they want nothing more than an online training
program. It is a check off the insurance box. It is a loose
bandage on a gaping wound. And, after an empowering
presentation covering real tactics, the participants always want
more.

It is astonishing what happens to the human body under
extreme amounts of traumatic stress, especially when facing
interpersonal violence. The sad reality is that violent situations
are dramatically escalating in the west. There is no assured way
to prevent them. No way to avoid them. No way to physically
prepare for them.

It is a problem that begs only one solution, a solution that
whispers to us in every facet of our lives: we must be confident
in who we are, in light of a greater vision.

My profession is unique because I get to discuss "Spiritual
Fitness" as a reality in the world. Workplaces don't allow it.
Businesses avoid it. Human resources are afraid of it. But when

a 12-guage Mossberg shotgun is pointed in your face, knowing the vision for your life is the only hope you have.

We must rely on a power that is even stronger than death.

I have felt this power elsewhere in the world, outside of the many violent circumstances I have been in. One of the strongest places I have felt it is in the blacksmith shop, refining average steel into something extraordinary through the intensity of the fire.

For the blacksmith, forging steel in the fire starts with a vision. It's not just a vision of what the steel will become. It's a vision of someone fearless with a passion to mold something beautiful.

Being prepared for the critical, unexpected, violent event is much the same. It starts with a true vision of yourself and a realistic understanding of this broken world. It requires that you internalize certain truths, develop certain characteristics, and decide ahead of time what role you will play. Will you be a bystander on the sidelines? A victim? A survivor? Or will you be forged through fire until you become fully alive, conditioned to respond effectively even in the worst moments?

Being prepared is dependent upon having this vision. Our vision gives us strength and forms the calluses on our hands. Those hands, our hands, can represent life or death, freedom or slavery. If we take the time to understand the dynamics of this vision, we will understand much more than emergency preparedness. We will finally see who we were meant to be.

So, what does it mean to become someone who lives without fear, a companion of peace throughout any trial? Is such a person possible? More importantly, is it possible for you to become that person?

I am not going to lie to you: being prepared is difficult. Physically, emotionally, and mentally, it is taxing. It takes energy, time, study, and sustained, arduous work. But having confidence that goes beyond death welded into the core of your being will redefine your soul.

As a blacksmith, I have never mentioned that I forge swords without an adventurous person's eyes lighting up with sudden fire. Here is what typically happens next: I invite the aspiring sword maker to my shop. After a hard day's work of sweat, blisters, and numerous burns, they are satisfied with the somewhat bent-out-of-shape railroad spike they endearingly call a "knife" and treasure for the rest of their days. They rarely come back to try again.

Human beings have certain traits that are common among us. One of the most interesting is our capacity to dream big, yet quickly trade in that dream for a quicker, less appealing reality.

We glimpse a vision. We feel a passion. Our hearts flicker. But the goal ends up being harder to achieve than we thought. It's funny how attractive the easy road seems when we face a difficult path. When dreams meet reality, reality tends to get the better of us.

In emergency preparedness, the reality is this: it is difficult to be fully alive and prepared for the unexpected, violent event. Like most important things, it takes dedication. But it is absolutely necessary in the day and age we live in.

Becoming the sort of man or woman who is ready for the unexpected is not a task to complete on your own. It requires more than a change of attire or the kind of untrained enthusiasm that motivates you to start carrying a knife on your ankle or a baseball bat in your office.

We're talking about a change of identity. To be an honorable man, a true warrior, is a dream most men once revered but have slowly lost as they became submissive, snared, and enslaved to lesser realities. It is a dream that many women have learned to stop searching for entirely, having been subdued to the point of abandoning their dreams and taking the more customary road.

As I look around, I realize something you already know to be true: the practice of becoming this type of person, someone defined by a greater vision, is a methodology lost to more ancient times.

Do you want to be prepared? Then you must wake up and become fully alive again. Do you want to find strength and hope, and a reality that has not been leached away by the mundane until only a mere whisper remains? Read this book. Then get up and change how you live. Let the sweat, heat, and pain of endurance renew and harden the best in you. The discipline of sticking to the task will give you more wisdom than will most other sources as you walk the long and hard road of life.

What follows in these pages is simple: I've outlined what it means to be ready for the unexpected, traumatic violent encounter. Not just how to correctly respond in an emergency, mind you, or how to survive one, or even how to prevent one. I'm talking about something more powerful: how to live every breath and heartbeat without fear. We will discuss regaining the vision that gives our hearts strength, even in critical moments. We will hammer out the character traits needed to sustain that long-lost vision. And we will study some basic strategic training that you'll need to correctly respond during the critical events which are becoming more common in our western world.

If you are eager to study crisis preparedness and tactical response, you may be tempted to skip right into the sections on training, situational awareness, and readiness for the violent event. I encourage you to read the first section of this book, *The Vision*, first. Real readiness comes from a real vision—a deep understanding of who you are, long before it has anything to do with emergency tactics.

Make no mistake, this vision is not required to survive the violent event, the major disaster, or the devastating tragedy. But is surviving your only aim? Is that the limit of your goal? We need a deeper vision, a vision that stirs us with power whether we will it to or not. In truth, very few people in this world have the strength to walk through life and into death dependent upon nothing but their own confidence. We need a vision that is more than ourselves. From my own experience, I can say that such a vision will make your personal growth swifter and more effective.

If you take all the sections of this book together, you'll find it to be a guide for the perilous journey of life.

I foresee an honest reader saying, "Come on! What's the point of all this personal growth stuff? I can find all I really need to know online, and the chances of my being in an active shooter situation are worse than getting struck by lightning! Why do I need this book?"

Well, I've been struck by lightning.

I've heard the bullets whistle over my head and watched them strike the people I know.

Like you, I've seen the darkness in the world and wondered what my part is to play in it. I've felt an indescribable yearning for something more. You don't have to be struck by lightning to realize you're not as in-control of this life as you'd like to think. The only question that remains is this: will we ignore the pain and brokenness in the world (and, truly, in ourselves), or will we turn and face it?

If you know, understand, and believe in a greater vision for your life, you can be effective even in the worst moments. Effectiveness in crisis cannot be predicted by appearance; it is predicted by whether you have a vision.

Section One: The Vision

Chapter One

The History of the Vision

Before we can be prepared for anything, we must have a vision. Not just a drive that motivates us, but a true life-force. For me, this vision started when I was eight. I was in the backyard, armed to the teeth with a machete and facing the insurmountable odds of a blackberry army. I knew then that I wanted to be a warrior; that I wanted to be valiant and able to act with a level head and strong hand even in the face of ridiculous odds.

I think it's safe to say that we *all* have a driving vision. In all of creation, mankind has the unique condition of never being satisfied with our environment. While other species fill particular niches and live contently within them, we question our creation and reach for the highest mountains. We imagine new worlds. And, unlike any other creature in the animal kingdom, we readily pass on those dreams and visions to future generations.

Because of the daunting challenges ahead, it's important for us each to define our own central vision before we start talking about emergency preparedness. I guarantee that you will encounter difficulties. You will get burned.

I remember being in the blacksmith shop when I was

younger, working on my very first sword. As I was hammering a 2000-degree piece of steel, my tongs broke. The steel jumped off the anvil and struck me in the face. It was so hot it melted into my skin, adhering there like a sticky piece of chocolate. A few weeks later, I dropped the same blade—this time heated to 1600 degrees Fahrenheit—to the bottom of a five-foot-deep quenching barrel filled with oil. The oil exploded into flame when I plunged the sword in, and I let it go in surprise. (To this day, I'm still not sure why I didn't expect that to happen.) As the sound of steel hitting the bottom of the barrel echoed in my ears, I thought, "Well, that's it then. All that for nothing." My sword would warp, bend, and possibly shatter as it cooled in the oil.

But I didn't give up. I reached chest-deep into that flaming oil, grabbed my sword, and tossed it to the master-smith behind me (who was laughing his coveralls off). Of course, my shirt was on fire. So was I. But—despite the fact that these circumstances proved that I was a slow learner—it was good. Why? In that moment, I was turning into a man worthy of holding the sword I was making. And that was, ultimately, what I sought.

Before you can act under pressure and against the odds, you must have a vision for yourself. If you and I are to be forged by fire into a worthy image, then we must come to terms with what that vision is: we must be able to articulate it. Who are you going to be when the violent encounter happens? When you have the choice to act or remain frozen, how will you know what to do? Will you even have a choice in those critical moments, or will you be a byproduct of your circumstances and habits?

The truth is simple: your vision defines you. And, if you look closely, the vision is bigger than you realize.

What this vision is can be hard for us to grasp and is always perilous to describe. It is deeper than character. More than drive. Bigger than the road we've walked down, no matter where that path has led. At its core, the vision stems from a yearning that we all have to be fully alive.

Our sense of this vision seems to fade just as quickly as it comes. It gets drowned out, strangled, and subdued. But all of us yearn to walk again into the fullness of it.

Having a sense of your true identity can be haunting if you don't look anything like how you imagine you should look to fulfill your vision. You have sensed the dream and traded it in for a lesser reality. But whether you've felt this way for a season or for as long as you can remember, I am here to challenge you with this truth: your life still has a worthy vision and a higher calling.

All of us have had days when the air seems to be clear around our minds. We see our path behind and the road ahead with stark clarity, and it fills us with confidence. But those are the easy days. Humans are forgetful; *we* are forgetful, especially after long and tedious trials. Yet we need to remember the true vision, even during the heat of a perilous encounter.

When I read ancient history, I am always amazed at just how much is dedicated to remembering. It is clear from antiquity that the issue of human forgetfulness is a particular problem we attempted to head off very early in our history. The first historical records were oral traditions, which were then followed by the world-changing developments of proto-writing, depictive writing, and, eventually, the written word.

The most ancient examples of proto-writing have no translation and their meanings remain unknown. Yet nearly all the writings and pictographs that *are* understood tell us rather disturbing things. Primarily, they agree that unexplainable, supernatural events have occurred among mankind. The most ancient histories of many regions describe a time when humans lived extraordinarily long lives and had blood that held a greater power. They tell of strange beasts, creation, world destruction, spirits of gods, demons, and angels, all intimately involved in our story.

Are all of these surviving documents fictional? Are all of

these tales exaggerated or untrue? Were they written by the "caveman" of our imaginations? The ancient rock-wielding barbarian?

These same "barbarians" designed the first weapons, invented smelting and casting, designed the ancient wonders of the world, and invented dykes and modern farming. They created cities of gigantic proportions and built marvels that still boggle the mind of modern engineering. These ancient peoples brilliantly used natural laws to make wonders we can still not duplicate. Only their largest works endure, and we can only speculate on the small-scale wonders which are completely lost.

It seems safe to assume that they were honest about the reality of the world they encountered.

This leaves a serious problem for the educated modern reader, as there needs to be an explanation for these documents and the long-forgotten history recorded within. The most logical answer is that these writings contain elements of truth, including their depiction of mankind involved in a greater story.

The modern assumption that belief in a higher power exists separate from history is dependent on a young and tenuous philosophy, rather than on reason. The strings of time whisper to us of a greater, older vision.

Here is a question you must come to terms with before you find yourself in the middle of a violent encounter: what is your part to play in history? To answer this question, you must seek the truth about who you are deep down in the bones of your soul. You need to do that now, *before* you start working on an emergency preparedness plan. I'll tell you why.

When I went through the police academy, I was surprised that the last week of training focused on preparing the spirit for a lethal-force confrontation. Spiritual preparation from a government institution? Really? Yes. In fact, I'll share with you what I recall one of my firearms instructors saying: "When you find yourself face-to-face with death or find yourself on the other side of a lethal-force confrontation, you won't have time to ask yourself the hard questions about your soul. You need to do that right now."

Answer those questions. Now.

PTSD stands for post-traumatic stress disorder. It is a psychological disorder that can be particularly acute when it comes from what is sometimes called "Combat Stress," which is more commonly known as interpersonal violence. When I train leaders and businesses on how to respond to active shooter situations or other traumatic violent events, I call the instigating trauma of PTSD "Code Black."

In short, Code Black is what happens to your mind when your nervous system gets overwhelmed. You experience tunnel vision. Auditory exclusion. Time seems to slow down. Most of you have experienced something along these lines when you've been in a car collision or experienced some other gut-wrenching, dangerous event.

When Code Black gets really bad or lasts for a long time, it can cause PTSD. Your mind starts to affect your body. You go into shock. Your heartbeat soars north of one hundred and seventy-five beats per minute. Your bowels void. You have flashes and dreams of the worst parts of the event, sometimes for the rest of your life.

Not long ago, a presentation I gave at a workplace violence conference inspired a woman in attendance to share her own recent experience with me. She felt ready to reflect on the fact that she had been shot twice during an active shooter event just two months earlier. Some of her other co-workers weren't as lucky. I remember she came up to me and said something quite remarkable: "People don't understand me anymore and I don't know why. What is scary is that I don't even know *myself* anymore. But I feel like I was woken up by what happened to me, and now I have to find out who I am again."

Are you seeing who you are clearly? When the safety and security of our world gets pulled aside and a raw, terrifying reality takes its place, I hope you have taken the time to sit down and ponder the real meaning of your life. Have you thought out your answers to the hard questions? The questions may be easy to ignore in our deceptively safe, secure, entertainment-based world. But we must answer them.

On the worst day of your life, the only thing worth knowing is who you are and what part you have to play in history. If you are going to truly be ready for the violent event, something must be different deep in your soul. You must be able to look into the eyes of your enemy and still remember the vision of who you are. That is the key element of a true warrior.

Chapter Two

The Master & the King

I don't have to look very hard into my bones before realizing that the vision of who I am is defined entirely by what I serve.

I met a man one time, albeit briefly, who was a servant of despair. He had let depression consume him, eating away at his soul until there was little else left in his life. He became so blinded by his misery that he decided to kill himself. He did so just after I had arrived to the 9-1-1 call. I don't know much of his story. I don't recall him saying much. I have a tough time remembering all the details, but I think he said "kill me" just before he blew his head off. I don't know anything else about him except that he had two young daughters who he left behind. The note in his truck was addressed to them.

I stayed up all night and into the next day after that event. Honestly, the more I thought about it the more I *wanted* to kill him. How could anyone be so blind? How could a man be such a coward, to abandon two little girls and his hope for the future?

But I know why: he was a man defined by what he served. He was a servant to despair and it consumed him.

A few years after, I had an opportunity to work alongside the Seahawks football team, assisting in their pre-game security detail. I remember meeting Marshawn Lynch, the fierce running-back who coined the term "Beast Mode." He's shorter than you would think, and he's a servant to power and fame.

I remember escorting him into his hotel the night before a home game. A family of three, clearly die-hard fans of the Seahawks, just happened to have selected the same hotel. The family's youngest was a little girl, no more than six years old. She was wearing a Marshawn Lynch jersey and had a little Seahawks football held tightly in her hands.

You wouldn't believe the size of her eyes when Lynch himself appeared in front of her. She ran up to him, six-year-old pigtails bouncing, with the biggest smile I have ever seen pasted on her face. She held out a marker and said, "Mr. Lynch, wud you sign my futbal peez?" It was adorable.

But Marshawn didn't even hesitate. He adjusted the gold earmuffs on his head and calmly told her to f*** off. His matching gold shoes carried him inside as she ran away crying.

Here is a man who is the hero of many. Countless fans would wish to be like him. But he is a servant to power and fame. It defines who he is and, at least in this instance, blinded him to what was truly powerful.

What is it that *you* serve? Because like it or not, you will become a slave to it.

Every person who undergoes trauma finds themselves at the mercy of whatever is the master of their life. For victims of violence, that master is often a self-perpetuating cycle of doubt and despair. It is a cage that is often called fear. For those who find themselves to be the delivery system of pain and hurt, it is a powerful likelihood that they are chained to an ill-formed master.

If you are going to do more than just survive in this world, you must have a vision. And that vision will come from whatever you have made master over your life.

Let me tell you when I saw my vision. It was in Guatemala in the early 2000s. Like in the ancient days, some third-world countries are still raw. The divide between the physical and spiritual isn't as muffled there, and sometimes a bigger vision breaks through.

I was in the middle of the Ixcan Jungle with a group of church-goers who were passionate about serving others. That was what defined them. I, however, was not defined by the same things. I was a selfish, prideful, teenage kid. In fact, the main reasons I ended up there were that I thought a few of the girls were cute and that I secretly hoped I would get the chance to meet a panther.

Many things on that trip troubled me deeply and challenged my perspective of the world. I saw unexplainable forgiveness, and I saw those with little more than a few chickens give all they had in the name of love. But nothing changed me as much as what happened on our third night in the jungle.

A storm had rolled in. A jungle storm. A monsoon. Ten times more rain than I had ever seen come down from the sky came down in a moment. Lightning cracked through the heavens and thunder rolled over the dense trees. We were staying in shacks; concrete walls climbing up to roofs made of chicken-wire and metal.

I felt called to go outside and see the power of the storm. So out I went, like a lamb being led to the slaughter. I didn't dare go beyond the awning, so I stood under the eaves in wonder as I watched the power of creation.

Now, to understand what happens next you must understand something about me: I was raised in a spiritually dry home. My father was an outspoken atheist and a good man, and my mother was a moralistic deist who wanted her kids to choose their beliefs for themselves. Whatever vision I had for my life was my own... which made it pretty small.

I didn't really care about what was true, so long as things didn't take much effort and benefited me in the long run. But what I had seen those past few days in Guatemala was difficult to swallow. In fact, it challenged my self-proclaimed identify so much that it hurt.

So, I did what perhaps some of you do when you are hurting: I blamed the author of the most important vision, the Master of Creation. In fact, I issued a challenge. I challenged the Master to reveal himself amidst the storm and show me his vision, if he existed at all. I challenged him to show up and prove me wrong. And I made the unspoken commitment that if he did, I would follow him.

I didn't even say the challenge aloud, I just said it in my bones, but I felt stupid right after I had thought it. And then nothing happened. The rain fell just as hard as before. The lighting crashed just as it had. I was about to turn and walk back inside when everything changed.

Now, the Master doesn't play by our rules and his plans aren't dictated by our time schedules. Yet, in this particular case, the Master had a very specific vision for my life. He was listening, and I was just exactly where he wanted me to be.

It's a common symptom of PTSD to remember deeply traumatic events from a third-person perspective. In this instance, the last thing I remember seeing from my own perspective was my hand, placed upon the wooden post holding up the awning above me.

The first thing to strike me was the silence. Utter, breathtaking silence where the tumult of the storm had just been. Time seemed to slow so dramatically that I recall wondering why I couldn't hear anything and why I couldn't move.

Then came the inverted field, like a one-hundred-million-lumen floodlight. As the light washed over the expanse of reality like a tidal wave, everything disappeared except for me. I was standing in the infinite expanse, alone. In the utter quiet. And I was terrified.

Just as I started to panic I felt it: the presence of the Master. The inescapable vision. In an instant, fear filled me like no other fear had or ever will again. I felt as if a supernova had exploded and I was at its epicenter, the focus of its intent. Like being hit by shockwaves, my self-security was ripped away, layer by layer. The small vision I had had of myself was destroyed, revealing a truth that I didn't want to face: I was not the master of my vision.

I had chosen to believe that I was in control of my own life. But in truth, I was far from in control. What I had believed about my own life, my very identity, was a lie. I realized that I was committed to a fake master—myself—and I was drowning.

In a moment that felt like a lifetime, I was forced to see a holy vision and it was too much for me to bear. Finding that I had been a slave to an imposter and that I did not have control over my own life left me staring into the face of death. How else can I put it? Despite all of my focus and intent, I was not on the right road. And worse than that, I found myself to be so far from the true vision and the True Master that I knew I would never be able to make it on my own. Not even close.

But the Master saw something within me, just as a father or mother sees so much potential in their son or daughter. He saw something I could never have envisioned, and he called me into it. I'm not sure if he spoke or not, but, right after accepting my hopeless fate, I remember feeling like this magnificent, hauntingly beautiful Power of Old abandoned his high place to come to me. Me, this wretched creature, this ungrateful mess deserving of death. Him, the Master of All, the steward of life, loving me and making me whole.

It was a reckoning of my soul. It was the beginning of my vision.

It took me almost three years to be able to tell that story. When I finally shared it, I had to have someone else read it for me because I couldn't speak. For six months after my return, I buried it, trying to forget its power. This is a common symptom of trauma. I still suffer PTSD from the experience: my hands tremble as I write and the broken images flash across my mind. A vision of my life was shown to me that I couldn't believe. But it was true.

Similar events have been recorded. Saul, blinded upon the road to Damascus; Daniel and his servants, cast down on the banks of the Tigris River, trembling like dead men; Ezekiel, unable to speak in the face of such mighty power: the vision of the Master.

As an emergency preparedness professional and as a student of psychology, I find it interesting how many people blame mass killings on mental illness. In fact, our culture has just two go-to explanations for mass killings: radicalism or mental illness. These explanations help us distance ourselves from the perpetrator and help us rationalize the destruction and pain.

Dehumanization is common, especially after a large-scale violent event that has caught the eye of modern media. But what kind of mental disorder can we blame these horrific acts on? Depression? Autism? Brainwashing?

Statistically, less than one in four mass shooters have a diagnosed mental illness. When an individual makes a purposeful, clearly articulated, logical plan for killing lots of people and then successfully executes that plan, it is not a sign of mental dysfunction. If anything, it represents a prominent capacity for critical thinking.

The right medication and some counseling sessions wouldn't have done anything to help Hitler reconsider his ways. It is the same for mass killers today. The success of a psychopath demonstrates that the individual is operating on all mental cylinders. They are very precise, rational, and articulate, fully equipped to succeed in our culture. But they choose not to.

It is terrifying because of how cold it feels. Whatever is master over these people's lives has consumed their being until they look, talk, think, and walk like normal, smart humans. But they are missing something. Something big. Something central to what separates humankind from the rest of creation. And it unnerves us.

It unnerves us because the absence of a greater vision

founded on goodness, love, and justice is not a mental disorder. It is just evil. And it comes in all different shapes and sizes.

Evil. Let's call it what it is.

Most people don't like talking about spiritual things. Most people don't like talking about death. Most people don't like talking about "force," or violence, or any kind of scary event. It makes them uncomfortable and for a good reason. All these things indicate the same reality: that at the end of the day, there is more happening in the world than our physical instruments can measure. Inherently, that means we are not in control. There is a vision greater than all of us. The question that remains is also the biggest question in emergency preparedness: what will you do about it?

Before you can truly be prepared, you need to come to terms with the fact that what we're truly talking about is the last day of your life. You don't know when it will come. You don't know if it will be fast or slow. But you do know that it is coming.

What will you do with this knowledge? Can you use the days you have left to bring life? Can you redeem the destruction around you, maybe even destruction you have wrought, into healing? Can you justify violence against another to protect yourself? To protect another? To protect someone undeserving?

At the end of the day, no matter how prepared you are, chances are good that your foe will have the jump on you. They will act before you can react, no matter how much training you have.

That begs a serious question that we all need to face and answer: are you ready to die?

With every firearms and lethal-force class I teach, I am forced to bring up this question about real life and real death—and everything else it reveals about how we are living our lives.

This whole messy business, from justifiable use of force to becoming fully alive in the critical encounter, starts with the vision of life and the question of death.

Exactly how big is your vision? Your vision is only as big as what you've made master over your life.

There is a greater vision. It's a loud, busy world, and we are a people who tend to focus on what is right in front of us. If there is an unseen battle between good and evil, it would be so very easy for it to be drowned out by our culture and by the mediocre stories we've been told. But every so often, a ray of sun breaks through the clouds.

Now, if you started thinking I was off my rocker the moment I began talking about a "master vision" and unseen forces, let's hit the pause button before we get any further. Articulating this vision is key to responding effectively to any crisis event in our lives. Yet emergency preparedness and traumatic, violent events are scary, and tying them directly to your soul probably wasn't what you were expecting this book to start off with. So let's base this conversation on something more widely accepted. In fact, let's go back to the foundation of every scientific principle we know to be true. That sounds like a much safer place to have this conversation, right?

Experts call that foundation quantum physics.

Quantum physics is, in short, the operating science that all other scientific theories get their facts from. It is the science of micro-matter, and it therefore effects every other scientific form which deals with matter. Which is <u>all</u> of science (and that's the truth of the matter).

One of my favorite principles in quantum physics is wave-particle duality. This is a principle that addresses the inadequacy of conventional scientific concepts. In fact, wave-particle duality goes so far as to state that our modern understanding of physical matter as distinct from raw energy is completely flawed. Translated, that means the collective, unspoken agreement between humans that physical things are separate from spiritual ones is complete nonsense.

The world is not flat.

Gravity is a real thing.

Evil is present in the world.

Physical and spiritual elements are tied together much more closely than you think.

Realize this: there is science in the art of seeking out and defining facts related to the master vision, so that those facts can be repeated and understood. This is why I love science. In its purest form, it is the search for truth through research. Yet science itself realizes the flaw in trying to explain things only from a physical perspective. Some things do not compute with a physical definition. Some things cannot be understood or quantified by a material measurement. Some things are not natural. It is a scientific principle.

Wait... really?

In science, there are varying levels of confidence regarding the true understanding of any given subject. These levels of confidence are reflected in the labels of different concepts. For example, the law of gravity is considered to be a pretty water-tight concept. We don't have much doubt it will change or is wrong, which is why it is called a law. Other concepts in science are labeled conjectures, hypotheses, and theories.

The most foundational of them all is a principle. A principle, by definition, is "a fundamental truth or proposition that serves as the foundational belief or behavior for a chain of reasoning." Principles are the truest form of fact, the bedrock of science as we know it.

So, let me share with you another scientific principle in quantum physics. Discovered by a man named Heisenberg in 1927, it is known as the indeterminacy principle. It states that the simultaneous measurement of two complementary variables is impossible. In fact, it states that the more precisely one scientific measurement is made, the more flawed the measurement of the other variable will be.

Basically, it contradicts classical physics as we know it in every shape and form.

Wait, wait, wait. Did science just tell me that, in some cases, by its very nature, it cannot be quantified? Did science just tell me that sometimes it cannot be predicted or measured? Does that mean that some things are not just physical but... supernatural?

This is the principle that prompted Einstein (who was a firm believer in the greater vision that I'm leading you toward in this book, by the way) to coin the phrase, "God does not play dice."

What he meant is simple. There is a real master, and this master has left a vision that we can find in our very atomic structure. But we will never be able to put it into an equation because, at its core, it is a supernatural vision. It is a vision that defies the laws of physics so thoroughly that it is a foundational principle.

The greatest minds the world has ever seen have tried to demonstrate through mathematics and science the existence of a single essence of force from which all other things derive their nature. Those of you that have researched quantum physics a little more know that I'm talking about string theory, or the "theory of everything." It is a supernatural vision that scientists are trying to explain with physical words. How ironic. We'll talk about some of these arguments more later, but be encouraged: Newton and Einstein asked the same questions about vision. They sought out the master of this vision and made him king over their life.

What is your vision? And perhaps even more importantly, who is your master?

Remember, you are defined by the master you serve, and that master will affect every element of your being. Will it be despair? Wealth? Power? The ability to live without pain? The ability to take life? A rock has the same power, loosed from a cliff, or a branch cast down by the wind. Those things are all empty ships floating on a windless sea.

Find the True Master and make him King over your life.

Honestly, at this point you need to either stop reading because you think I'm a lunatic or believe that this whole thing—your life and the lives of all the people around you—just might sit upon the shoulders of a more ancient, more powerful vision. A more ancient battle. A greater story of good and evil. And you need to believe that this vision includes you as a vital element to the story of the world.

You have a vision for your job. You have a vision for your family. You have a vision about what you'd like for dinner.

But what about *you*? What is your purpose? *Why* do you want to be prepared for the violent emergency event?

If we can't articulate this as well as we can articulate what we'd like to have for dessert, then we've discovered the first step we must take on our journey toward emergency preparedness.

Ancient history is full of people searching for their purpose and, coincidently, the True Master. Across continents and times, seeking out the Master has been a fueling fire in history because it is the start of the vision.

If you can sift through the myth, it's remarkable how similar ancient stories become the further back you go. But that's the tricky part about finding the Master, of course: sifting through the myth. Our minds are interesting things. Hard to open and easily overwhelmed.

Consider the ancient Israelites and their search for the Master. From where I sit, it's easy to read their story and think that, as a whole, the ancient Israelites were about as smart as a bag of hammers. As the story goes, the Master showed up to them on several occasions, each time to teach them the vision of their life. Yet, even after being told the Master's vision directly, they abandoned it, preferring to receive their vision from various meaningless objects... sometimes just days after receiving the vision.

What?! *Days* afterward?! After receiving the vision *directly* from the Master? You've got to be kidding. How can anyone be *that* forgetful?

But the more I think about my own story, the more I see that forgetting is deeply ingrained in us as a race. The Master has intervened in miraculous ways several times over the years in my life; yet, unless I intentionally try to remember and document them, they just fade into my usual routine. I have a feeling it's like that for you, as well. It is for this reason that I think mankind originally invented pen and ink, so that when our minds are not strong enough to recall the vision of our forefathers, we can go back and re-remember it.

Our culture has forgotten what a greater vision looks like. Just the other day, I was interviewing a twelve-year-old girl who found herself on the wrong side of a "sexting" situation. That is to say, she responded to a boy at school who asked for a picture of her naked. When I asked her why she would send such a picture, this young girl simply shrugged.

"That's just how it is. Everyone does it," she said.

That might be how it is. But it is not how it should be. We desperately need to remember the greater vision for our lives.

Chapter Three

The Dividing Line

Realize that you have great power in your hand: both the ability to do much good and the tendency to do nothing at all. The ancient Celts would say, "Never give a sword to a man who can't dance." They would be right.

I think those ancient Celts understood the fact that before anyone is ready to wield great power, they should be able to see what is right and good in the world. Like the ancient samurai, the Celts—those barbarous pixies of northern Scotland—understood the fundamental tie between the human heart, the human mind, and the human hand.

Why is it that when you experience a severe emotional loss, you feel physically sick? When you are surrounded by three men in a dark alley, why is it hard to think? Why is it so easy to continue drinking after a long week, even when you know it will hurt in more ways than one?

We have a vision. A vision of who we are made to be, regardless of the circumstances we find ourselves in. Something strong, something beautiful, something reliable. But we often find ourselves to be just the opposite. When push comes to shove and we're caught between the hammer and the anvil, we give in. We don't act when we should. We act when we shouldn't. And we regret it. We hide from it. We settle for less.

And we know we were made for more.

This knowledge begs a simple question: where does our vision come from? Is this mystical vision a cultural phenomenon or a product of our survival instincts? Could it be something more? Something greater?

Before we can trust ourselves to act with strength and honor in the worst moments, we have to know and understand the vision of our own life. We must identify and name that vision. And we must understand that it comes from a greater source of power than ourselves.

Humans are complicated, our design unparalleled. The first record we have of groups of people who seemingly rejected the idea of a supernatural vision for their lives begins around 600 AD. From our records, it seems these groups were sporadic and isolated. Even now, less than two percent of the world agrees with the idea that there is no Master, no vision from a Maker, and that our design and the world's design happened by chance. They think there is no objective vision. This is roughly about the same percentage of people who believe the world is still flat.

Unfortunately for these folks, the mathematical (and objective) odds aren't in agreement.

Imagine making a sword in a blacksmith shop. What is the probability of the initial, unworked piece of steel creating the fire, the forge, the tools, and the sword through small, random changes... and no blacksmith?

Really? Do I even need to ask that question? Apparently, I do. The answer would likely be the same no matter who you ask: it would be very unlikely, with a lot of zeros behind the odds. And a sword is much less complicated than a human being.

But the question has created a huge, uncomfortable rift in our culture between "creationists" and "evolutionists." Like most problems, the division is the worst part about it, and I'm grateful to not have to disagree with either side.

Once you realize that supernatural principles naturally tie

into everyday ones, things get a whole lot simpler and we can start to make sense of our vision. Love is not just a chemically driven state of emotion that entwines into a culturally driven expectation: it is the giving of all you are for another. Faithfulness is not just an obligation driven by subjective opinion, shame, and the avoidance of regret. It is a covenant between a lesser reality and a greater one. Discipline is not a monkish approach to a philosophical problem. It is a conscious decision to walk on the high road of the Master's vision, even when difficulty presents itself along the way.

These particular traits are not evolutionary, they are not wholly scientific, and many of them are not even reasonable. They are supernatural. If you haven't considered the real fact that there is an unseen spiritual reality that explicitly ties into our physical reality, then you need to open your eyes. Do some real research. Look at the connection between the mind, heart, and body of man.

Let me put this into context. If you want to be prepared for what might be the last day of your life, you should have already wrestled with the question of what lies on the other side of the dividing line (death). Going further, if you can't see right from wrong, how can you articulate when interpersonal violence is evil and when it's not?

We need to have a guiding line, an objective reality of good and evil, before we decide which battles are worth fighting for. We need to be able to dance before we can wield a sword.

The first part of training is seeing the wrong around you in contrast to the vision of righteousness the Master has forged into your heart.

There are two different kinds of fundamental truths in the world. The first is called subjective truth. This truth is based on the idea that if enough people agree on something, it is true. The second kind of truth is objective truth. This truth is simply... true. No matter what anyone thinks. Mathematics is one of the most basic objective truths in the world. 2+2=4. I don't care if you think it equals five. I don't care if ninety-nine percent of the world thinks 2+2=5. They are all wrong.

How do I know when something is worth fighting for? Arguing over? Dividing over? Defending to the point of death? This is a brutal question, and it is key to understanding the vision of our lives. It is one that certainly must be answered before we start talking about readiness for the violent event.

Subjectively, knowing what is worth fighting for is not hard. The pyramid of subjective truth ends with our legal system. Look at your local state laws regarding justifiable use of force. You'll notice that (unless you're a sworn officer) you're not *required* to intervene in any circumstances, even when others are getting hurt around you and you have the ability to stop it. Subjectively, do we have an obligation to do right? To intervene when we can?

Our laws answer this for us: no. There is no objectivity to this subjective truth. Yet I often hear people say, "Well, morally, I would *have* to do something..."

Yes. They're right. That is called hearing the whispers of an objective vision.

Objectively, determining where to make your stand on the matter of "truth" is the ultimate question and the foundation of our vision. The subjective opinions of our culture still reek with the echoes of objective reality. They always have. Laws are built upon ethics. Ethics are built upon morals. Morals are built upon objective truth.

If there is no objective, supernatural reality of good and evil, then there is no battle worth fighting for.

Once you affirm that there is an objective reality—a supernaturally right vision for you and for the world—you'll become increasingly aware that there is something seriously wrong: we, as a human race, are very far away from that vision. And generally speaking, we're moving in the wrong direction.

An active shooter is defined by the FBI as an individual who kills—or attempts to kill—people in a populated area. Since the turn of the 20ᵗʰ century, active shooter events have increased within the united states by over 600 percent. In case you didn't hear that: I said *600 percent*, and that definition doesn't include any mass shootings involving targeted victims, domestic violence, drug activity, or terrorism. Which means it is a low-end estimate. Prior to the 20ᵗʰ century, we had a few mass killings each year within the U.S. Now we have more than one every day.

And it doesn't stop with the restrictive FBI definition of "active shooter."

Statistically, four to six women are going to be murdered by their significant other in the next 24 hours.

Violent crime in Chicago this year alone is going to produce more deaths than the total number of soldiers lost by the U.S. in any war in the last twenty years.

One out of four people you know have been sexually assaulted. Or will be.

Nine out of ten men you know between the ages of 15 and 30 are using pornography.

And most of these numbers come from self-reported statistics, which means they are low-end numbers.

This shouldn't be a surprise. If I asked you to stop reading right now if you've lived a perfectly safe life, I'm convinced I wouldn't lose a single one of you. Honestly, I'm willing to bet either you or someone you love has been the victim of a violent event. Assault. Domestic Violence. Home Invasion. Molestation. Robbery. Carjacking.

It happens all the time, and it's getting worse.

In 2014, a young man walked into Otto Miller Hall on the Seattle Pacific University campus armed with an over-under shotgun and a large hunting knife. This man heard what he described as the voice of Satan and the Columbine killers telling him to send people to hell. He killed one and wounded two others before he was subdued by Jon Meis.

Now I just happen to be an alumnus of Seattle Pacific University, and Jon's older brother was a good friend while I attended. I met Jon several years before the incident and, I'll be honest, I thought he was a complete geek. He could probably kick my butt on an Xbox, but that's about it. And I was right insofar as Jon had zero tactical training, no combat experience, and he made a variety of tactical mistakes during the incident that could have gotten him killed.

But it didn't matter.

What Jon did have was a vision. He had a vision of the Master engraved upon his heart. He knew the truth about himself and it gave him context for how to address the brokenness of the world.

I called his brother, Chad, when I saw the news coverage. And I'll never forget what Chad told me.

"It was Jon," Chad said. "Jon took him down. Jon stopped the shooter."

"How?" I asked in disbelief. "How did he do it?"

"I don't know," Chad replied. "I don't know. He was filled with the Power of the Spirit. It's crazy."

Yes. That is crazy.

What if I told you that no matter how much training you've undergone, it wouldn't be enough? No matter how strong you were, it wouldn't matter? All the time you just spent preparing, a waste.

If you are battling against someone who believes in a supernatural vision and you don't, you're already fighting against the odds. But for someone with vision, death is not the end. It is just the beginning. And Jon Meis is the kind of man who has that vision.

Our battle is not just a battle of flesh and blood. There is evil in the world. We have an enemy who strikes much deeper, who threatens not only our physical lives and the lives of those we love, but our ability to see the Master's vision.

From my studies and from what I have seen in my own life,

the evidence is overwhelmingly in favor of two fundamental, objective truths. First, there is a master who has a vision for your life, and who loves and cares for his creation. Second, there is an enemy, a real force of evil that has chosen to hate the vision of the Master.

Coincidentally, that means the enemy hates you and the people you love.

The battle between this good, enduring, true vision and this unspoken evil enemy affects our whole being: heart, mind, and body. Each area needs training to be able to stand firm in the time of crisis. Before we address this concept any further, I want to introduce three basic categories that readers might find themselves in. You may not be categorized here, and that's fine. But some of you will identify with one of these camps: the safe, the broken, and the overwhelmed.

The safe:
You've led a relatively easy life. It might not have started that way, but it sure is how things are now. Sure, your modern-day life is full of risks and adventures. Like taking out the trash, talking with your relatives over the phone, and going to the gym. You might believe in the Master or you might not. Who cares, really? Either way, it's more of a side-note to your relatively safe life. And you know what? You've earned it. You've got things pretty well figured out and you are happy with your routine.

The broken:
You have lived a life that seems comparable to hell itself. You are addicted, abused, and unappreciated. You are broken and you know it, and there doesn't seem to be anything you can do to get yourself out of where you find yourself stuck.

The overwhelmed:
It doesn't matter what you believe: you are in over your head.

You don't have enough time, and things are starting to fall apart. Screw this. It won't matter, anyway. It never does.

Regardless of what camp you find yourself in or which combination of camps you've been in for the duration of your life, I need to tell you something that is going to make a lot of sense—and even more sense the more you think on it. You have an enemy. This isn't some mystical cloud of evil that floats around. This enemy has a purpose and a history that stretches all the way back into the ancient times. He wants to take you out of the fight, and he's going to attack your whole being to try and destroy your vision.

Sun Tzu, the ancient author to whom *The Art of War* is attributed, makes two necessary and obvious claims.

1. "Do not engage an enemy more powerful than you, and if it is unavoidable, engage them on your terms."
2. "If you are ten times stronger than your enemy, surround them. If double, divide them. If weaker, avoid them."

The first step of effective training is to get a grip on the reality of the world. There is a battle, and you need pick which side you are on. There is a supernatural good vision. And there is a supernatural evil enemy. And that enemy wants to end you.

The history of this enemy I do not know. Popular opinion reflects ancient history and seems to say that this creature was once a powerful spiritual being who had been in line with the good vision. But then, through the Master's gift of free will, this thing took the vision into its own hands, twisting it to serve his own desires and corrupting the hearts of mankind along the way.

Regardless of how the enemy came about, or what exactly this enemy is, it is critical to understand we have one. In fact, according to popular belief, we are living in the enemy's self-proclaimed capital: the physical world. This puts everything into an understandable context. This isn't la-la land. It is the enemy's encampment. If you don't believe me, turn on the news.

Here is where I am going with this: we need to understand that the darkness we see in the world isn't the fault of climate change, poor political leadership, or technology. Evil taints everything it touches, even things that were created for good. Like humankind.

The enemy of the world thinks you are dangerous to his mission and he wants to take you out of the fight. This enemy has been around for a very, very long time. His strategy is paramount. His delivery vicious. And he knows a lot about you and mankind. Since the ancient days, the enemy's strategy has been refined to better attack us by taking footholds in our culture.

For the "safe," the enemy has convinced you that there is no battle worth your interest. You are such a threat that he has had to pull the trump card: avoidance. He makes you think the battle is over—that you have earned a respite—or that it never even existed to begin with.

For the broken, the enemy has thrown all of his weight upon you. He has tried to crush the very life from your lungs so that you might throw in the towel and back away from the fight, accepting defeat.

For the overwhelmed, the enemy is melee attacking you. Feinting here, thrusting there, trying to surround you with so many small wounds that you bleed out upon the battlefield.

We'll talk more specifically about some of these attacks later on, but for now I want us to simply realize that *we are actually being attacked*. Have you ever read a story or watched a movie where you, as the audience, see the bad guy coming for the main character before they do? You want to reach out and shake that character. You want to yell, "Turn around! He's right behind you!"

Well, the enemy is right behind you. He's been trying to pin you down for a long time. He's been refining his strategy on how to subdue you. And now he finally thinks he's getting close. Open your eyes and see the reality of the world you live in.

Victims and aggressors in traumatic events are best understood in context, and that context always hints toward their vision and the master over their life. We are dealing with an entire culture, a vast and mighty forest, that is perpetuated by pain. Saturated with brokenness. And it's getting worse. So how do we break the cycle of evil?

I know how, and we are going to get there. Later.

For the moment, I'm going to pause this part of the conversation, leaving the question unanswered. Know that you have a part to play in this battle for good, for peace. A full life is truly the context for preparedness, so we've walked this far.

But I'm not going to help you identify this vision any more than I have, or identify a name for the True Master, the maker of the vision. It's a journey you must walk down, no doubt about it. It certainly is critical to know before you face the dark of a traumatic event, or raise children, or do anything that has real value. But it is a journey you must choose on your own.

You need to be able to articulate your vision and decide which side of the fight you are on. And if you think you are just "not going to pick," then the enemy has done his work all too well.

Seek the Master and search for a vision that will be a solid foundation when the violent encounter happens. Wake up and seek the vision that will be the essence of *you*. Do it in spite of where you've been. Do it in spite of where you think you are. Do it before you go into battle. Do it before you find yourself unwillingly immersed into the pain of this broken world. Ask yourself the hard questions, because it is easy to get distracted when things get hot and the sparks begin to fly.

Once you've studied your history, visited the tough places in the world, and taken a close look at the vision for your own life, you'll realize that we need to do something. Regardless of what stage of life you find yourself in, or the specifics of who you think the Master is, we need to put up a fight. We need to resist the darkness in the world. Now it's time to start training.

Section Two: The Battle

Chapter Four

Understanding a "Win"

Up until this point, we have been naught but visionaries. Our discussion would be as aptly suited to a sofa and a half glass of good scotch as it would be to a seminary hall. But now we need to suit up, crack those knuckles, and get ready. It's time to jump into action.

What kind of action is most appropriate when talking about active killers? Or, to put it simply, how do you *win* in an active shooter situation?

I hear all sorts of answers when I ask this question. Survive. Kill the bad guy. Defend yourself. Have no one get hurt. Go home at the end of the day.

Those are all good answers, but none of them are "wins." The reality is this: if an active killer event happens, there is deep trauma that wreaks havoc within the community—even if everyone survives, even if the killer gets taken into custody.

The only way to win in an active killer situation is to prevent it from ever happening to begin with.

If we're going to talk about the real win (*prevention*), then we need an understanding of how human beings process anger, frustration, and pain. And, who knows? Maybe we'll even gain some insight into our own vision while we do so.

People's processing cycle is most easily understood within what I call the "theory of escalation." This theory puts into context aggression, the justification of pain, and holistic ability.

Aggression:

Aggression is demonstrated in an unbelievable number of contexts. Aggression can be healthy, it can be enslaving, or it can be hurtful. Fortunately, aggression is pretty easy for us to recognize.

I want you to look over the diagram below and enter into the appropriate category your best guess for each of the following questions.

If you had to guess, what percentage of aggression is demonstrated through physical, aggressive behavior such as killing, punching, biting, or fighting?

If you had to guess, what percentage of aggression is demonstrated through verbal aggressive behavior such as shouting "Jerk!", "Pin-Head!", or "I'm going to come back and get even with you!"?

If you had to guess, what percentage of aggression is demonstrated through non-verbal aggressive behavior such as posturing, stance, hand motions, or eye motions?

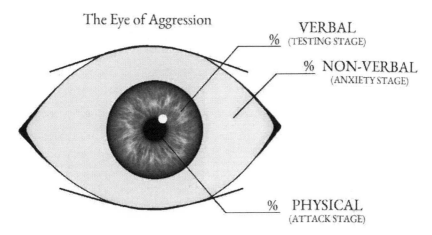

Image 1. The Eye of Aggression

Let's look at the answers.

Physically aggressive behavior comprises less than *three percent* of all aggressive indicators. This is fantastic, and I'll tell you why: because if we're trying to prevent physical aggression from happening, there are a lot of other areas that *aren't* physical where we can get involved. That sets us up for a win if we're ready to take intervening action early on.

Verbal aggressive behavior comprises about *seven percent* of all aggressive indicators. And while this number seems surprisingly low, we've all been there. We know what it is like when we don't get our way, or we're upset, or we want a problem to go away. So, what do we do? We let other people know there is a problem!

Non-verbal aggressive behavior comprises more than *ninety percent* of all aggressive indicators. Whether you like it or not, when you're upset, experiencing pain, or undergoing frustration, your body language changes to reflect your demeanor.

The target of aggression shown in Image 1 is important for

us to chew on. First, and most importantly, understand that no one has ever simply woken up in the morning with the novel concept of wanting to hurt as many people as possible. People do not just "snap," though you hear the term often in the news.

People have real needs. All people. And when those needs aren't met or a situation seems impossible to overcome, it creates fear, anxiety, and frustration. That anxiety can build over time (and sometimes rather quickly) and spill over into verbal testing. Toeing the line. Searching for a reaction, a response, anything that would bring recognition and healing to the unsatisfied need.

If the need is still not met, some people continue to escalate into physical violence. We'll come back and talk about this more during the next section. For now, I just want to get you thinking. Thinking about what these percentages mean.

They mean that we have time to intervene early, meet needs, and prevent violence. *That* is a win.

Justification:

Every problem comes with pain because pain (or the avoidance of it) seems to be the root of most problems. But is pain abnormal? Does hurt, even if it is deep, cause us to spontaneously abandon the values that shape our lives? A wise friend once said, "The kind of person you are does not show itself during the easy times in your life. It is during the storm that the real you comes forth."

Just the other day, I was turning a beautiful wooden bowl on the lathe. It was an intricate piece, covered with marvelous knots and grain patterns. As I was turning off the machine, the tool in my hand nicked the rotating bowl's edge. The bowl, rotating at about 2250 RPMs, immediately shattered. In an instant, several scenarios crossed my mind. One involved throwing an item across my shop. Another involved a garbage can. Another involved wood glue, several clamps, and many days of unanticipated patience.

It is entirely normal for human beings to experience a problem, fantasize about solutions, effect an action plan, prepare for that plan, and then carry it out. In fact, if we didn't have this problem-solving capability, we wouldn't be able to remedy any of our problems!

Generally speaking, violence can be broken into two generic categories: targeted aggression and reactive aggression. While both types can lead to critical violent moments, targeted aggression is by far the more dangerous when it comes to active killers. Why? Because action within goal-setting behavior *requires* justification. Reactive aggression is an unthought-out response. Targeted aggression comes from a very dangerous cycle of events, demonstrated below.

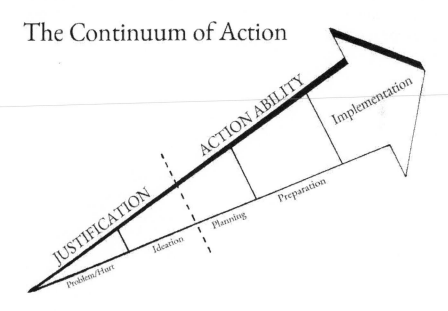

The Continuum of Action

Image 2. The Continuum of Action

Whether we're talking about turning a wooden bowl, an intimidated student trying to regain control, or a person trying to be sexually accepted, the cycle of behavior starts with the justification process. We unconsciously hold our actions to the standard of a greater vision.

When I started studying justification, I was startled by how much of it I recognized in my own life. I've caught myself driving home from work, fantasizing about a conversation I might have with a neighbor, my spouse, or a co-worker. I've been shocked to find myself planning how to get what I need, even if it is merely a pre-thought-out comment to get an edge in an argument.

I'm sure you've never done anything like that....

It is amazing to me just how quickly small molehills can turn into mountains when we get focused on a smaller vision.

All of us attempt to justify the means of our actions, even if that justification is simply, "I don't care anymore." If a person does not perceive that options exist, or if clear boundaries and consequences aren't in place, extreme justification becomes easier. If ability also exists, then extreme justification results in a higher likelihood of extreme action.

Holistic ability:

Holistic ability is not action ability, which consists of the resources and capability to commit an atrocious act. Holistic ability is something that affects any and all individuals present in a traumatic event: both victims and aggressors.

In any major disaster, there are three distinct elements of mankind that are affected. Each one plays a role in preparedness, action, and recovery.

Image 3. The Wholistic Nature of Mankind

The Mind: The mind is the "eye" of man, keeping us focused and sharp. This piece is vital for self-control, discipline, and wisdom, and has been developed and refined through thousands of years of learning and passed-down knowledge. It is the mind that allows us to think tactically before battle, remain focused during it, and learn after it.

The Heart: The centerpiece of our lives, the heart is the vision the Master has for you. This is reflected in what you are passionate about. It is your drive, your rhythm, and your heartbeat. The heart is why you get up in the morning and why you breathe every day. It is why you will train and why you care, even when things get hard.

The Body: The body is the delivery system. The mind and the heart are enough, for some missions, to define an individual. But you cannot exist without that which sets you apart from the rest of physical creation. It is the piece you must train in order to deliver the mission that the Master has spoken to your mind and heart.

Just like the components of a car, each of these elements is uniquely connected to the rest. Whether you lose a tire, a water pump, or your gas pedal, the end result is still the same. The car has broken down.

I am always amazed by what happens to me when I stop eating. Honestly, I can get so focused on the task at hand that I just forget to eat. Yet when I neglect my body, my mind becomes dull and my heart dim. It's the same thing the other way around: when your heart is upset by the loss of a loved one, it effects your whole being. You lose your appetite. You stop caring.

Understanding these elements is critical in tactical training. If I can intentionally upset a key element within my opponent, I gain a foothold within his entire bodily system. Unfortunately, this is also true for us. When the enemy gains a foothold, it affects our whole life and shakes our vision to its core. This is just one more reason to build our lives on the bedrock of an unshakable vision.

The point is, each one of these pieces of identity creates who you are. If you leave out the hilt of a sword, you don't have a sword. You have a machete. If you dull the point and edge of a sword and lengthen its handle, you don't have a sword. You have a shovel.

You must train, sharpen, and forge each aspect of you to become complete. You must be vigilant, focusing on each in turn and all as a whole. You must guard them, for they are the wellspring of life. Remember this: a sword hanging above your mantle is different from a sword wielded in battle by a trained warrior. One matters no more than a decorative vase. The other determines the course of history.

Ironically, being prepared for a traumatic, violent event requires a material that is very similar to that of a sword. The more layers of steel you have, the better you'll hold up in the stress of combat. Even if you make a perfect sword, it will not withstand the stress of battle if it's made out of aluminum. The most effective blades have the ability to hold a hard edge while retaining a soft core to bounce back when hit hard.

You are made from good, solid material. You have, very naturally, the ability to be hard and to be soft; to be loving and to be vengeful; to be faithful and to be true. But, unlike a sword, you have been given a choice. A sword cannot see itself, nor imagine its place in creation. It does not fathom its maker or ask questions when ordered to kill. It does not feel regret, guilt, or joy.

But you are different.

You and you alone have a choice that must be made, or it will be made for you. Will you seek out the truth? Answer the hard questions? Will you find your design and allow yourself to be unmade and then remade in the fire?

You get to choose what kind of person you will become. And if you don't choose, you will remain and die in the same state that you currently find yourself in: a lump of carbon.

Chapter Five

Preparedness, Awareness, & Action

Let's assume that we have the fundamentals figured out. We are seekers of the truth. We know who we are. We understand the vision for our lives. We are willing to invest energy and time, which are so valuable to us, in walking down the road of life as prepared as we can be. We understand the importance of training our mind, our hearts, and our bodies as a whole unit. We know prevention and early intervention is the only way to win.

If that all sounds intimidating, don't trade in the Master's vision for a lesser reality and an easier road. Becoming an individual who is truly prepared for the emergency event is a path that requires discipline and dedication. Most likely, these characteristics won't fall into your lap, just like you won't be able to do a spinning heel kick when you wake up tomorrow morning. Keep training, keep pursing the truth.

Now it's time to start talking about the reality of combat.

There is an enormous difference between training for a battle and being in one. Every once in a while, I have someone walk into my training facility and say, "Sorry, I can't train. I would just end up killing you." Typically, these kinds of comments come from former military professionals who tried to make it into special ops but dropped out. The reality is, if you are going to learn how to effectively use your body, mind, and heart in battle, you must be able to train.

Training takes practiced discipline. When training for the most dangerous situations, such as when training CQB (close quarters battle), you need utter control of your body and your weapon system. You have to be able to move at 100% speed with enough emotional and physical control to NOT seriously injure your training partner or accidently fire your weapon. Only the professionals have the ability to train at 100% speed while executing enough discipline to still consider it training.

But why do we train? Obviously, we train so that we can effectively execute the same mentality, the same moves, and the same heart-set when things go bad. We call this preparedness. You have a plan. You know the moves. When the building catches on fire, you know what to do. When the active shooter fires off the first shot, you know your options and you've practiced them.

The basis of tactical preparedness is training. If you can't or don't train, you better have a strong prayer-life. You'll need it.

Preparedness is based on two simple principles that form the foundation of our training: awareness and action ability.

When the FBI conducted their 2013 study on active shooter events in the United States, they dug up a lot of really good information. There is one nugget of wisdom that got buried in their analysis and doesn't get touched on very much, but it is one of my favorites. They found a correlation between denial and high-fatality active shooter incidents. Basically, they discovered that in a real crisis event, the vast majority of people just can't believe it is really happening.

I've seen it time and time again, in real life and in training. A gunshot goes off and the students in the communal area think it's a balloon, someone playing a practical joke, a water-heater exploding... anything but what it actually sounds like: a gun.

During my training courses, I often include what are called

"mock scenes." Mock scenes are designed to simulate real-life events, and they help our trainees struggle through this mentality.

Just recently I had one of our group leaders go through a domestic violence mock scene. The scene started off just like any other day: at the bus stop, checking his cell phone, thinking about work, wondering what's for dinner. Most of the time, that's all people see. It is their focus. And they miss the car in the parking lot, about ten cars away, violently shaking back and forth.

What is so startling to me is that most people, *even if they realize it is happening,* come up with an excuse. They justify a reason to avoid getting involved. "Oh, I'm sure they are just changing out the tire." What?! "Maybe they are just really excited about something." Uh-huh. "Maybe they are just having a bad day." Duh.

This happens in training AND in real life. It is astounding to watch.

At this point, most people do one of three things: they remain oblivious to what is happening, they ignore and cultivate an imaginary excuse for what is happening, or they rush in.

All three are wrong solutions.

As guardians of the vision the Master has laid upon our hearts, we must mutually be prepared for the worst, be aware of what is happening, and then be able to correctly transition into action. These three steps are the basis, the solid foundation, for every tactical crisis situation you will ever face.

We've already spent some time talking about how to prepare our mind, body, and heart for the crisis moment: we have to see and believe the vision. We have to be rooted in objective truth. We must come to terms with the fact that there is a seen and unseen enemy. We train so that we are ready to protect the vision.

The next step is to understand situational awareness and

action ability.

When training for situational awareness, it is easiest to break things down into color codes.

White. Yellow. Orange. Red. Black.

These five (originally four) symbolic colors were first developed by Col. Jeff Cooper in his essay, "Mental Conditioning for Combat." They have since evolved to become one of the principle tools of awareness training.

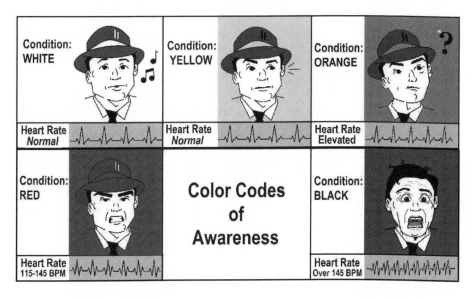

Image 4. Color Codes of Awareness

White signifies a completely safe environment (or at least an environment you think is completely safe) where you are calm and oblivious. Zero awareness. Zero alertness.

Unfortunately, this is where most of the world is *all the time*. Oblivious to the reality. Get off your cell phone and have a real conversation. Stop playing Call of Duty three hours a day or more. I hate to break it to these folks, but an online ranking has nothing to do with the Master's vision for your life. Sorry. You are missing the real world.

People playing games like Call of Duty feel the vision and want the call, or they wouldn't be playing. But all they're doing is improving the dexterity of their thumbs. Time to put aside the easier, electronic, *fake* reality and become fully alive.

I once saw an individual driving down the freeway smoking, eating a sandwich, putting on makeup, and talking on the phone. It was a stick shift. Talk about being in condition white.

On the whole, condition white is not a bad thing. From time to time, I find someone in a training course who tells me they think *no one* should be in condition white. Ever. They are wrong. In fact, the more you train and the more battles you fight, the harder it is to find yourself in condition white *even if you want to.*

The fact that it becomes harder to find condition white is part of the reason you shouldn't go into battle until you understand the vision of the Master. You have to be able to come back home. You have to be able to find rest and let the Master lead your soul along quiet waters. The difficulty of coming back home without understanding this vision explains why police officers have astronomically high divorce rates and the 4th-highest suicide rate in the United States.

With every good thing, there is a balance. Having no condition white is detrimental, but too much condition white is really bad because you don't see anything happening around you. This balance applies in combat, in our spiritual lives, and in our closest relationships.

Yellow signifies a normal, tactical state of awareness.

This does not mean you are a ninja, walking around everywhere in combat boots and x-ray goggles (though I love tactical boots, don't get me wrong). You are simply aware that we have a real enemy who seriously wants to destroy the vision of a full life for you and for others. You know the truth, you've prepared yourself, and you are out in the real world.

For most people in the United States today, just getting out in the real world is the biggest hurdle. Because it is so easy not to. It is so easy to live in a completely (or so you think) safe and secure environment. Maybe this has to do with our level of wealth, or our level of technology, or the level of safety preparedness our country implements on our behalf without our knowledge. I'm not sure. But it is a real problem.

The only reliable statistic that correlates with violent events is people. Anytime you are around people, there is a risk of violence. The great thing about being in code yellow, aside from feeling aware, is that it makes you a very undesirable target. Most bad guys take the path of least resistance. If you are aware and alert, you are already separating yourself from the majority.

There is a very small number of people in my life who are uncomfortable with me carrying a firearm around them. Anywhere, really, but particularly in their house. They know I always do, so they very specifically ask me to leave it behind on those occasions when I'm at their residence.

This drives me absolutely nuts. It is a classic response from someone living in condition white.

Well, your home is a safe place, right? Why would you need a superior weapon there? What are the chances of a real, dangerous threat happening in your home?

On June 21, 2013, a woman was in her suburban New Jersey home making breakfast while her 3-year-old daughter watched TV on the couch. Her 18-month-old baby was asleep upstairs. Just another typical day.

Suddenly, from the garage, entered Mr. Criminal—who I will not give the honor of naming. He just happened to be passing through town. Mr. Criminal walked right in through the garage door and, in front of her daughter, beat this woman into near unconsciousness. He choked her, kicked her across the room multiple times, and threw her down a flight of stairs before grabbing random valuables from the house.

Then he left. The whole thing was caught on a nanny cam the mother had set up downstairs.

I still remember the first time I saw that video. After many hours of prayer, I decided to share it with my wife. She is a fighter and a warrior, but we all get complacent. I can't tell you the number of times I have chased a criminal through someone's backyard. Into a random person's house. I shouldn't have to tell you the statistics on how many active shooter incidents happen in your neighborhoods, your apartment complexes, at the park, or while driving to work.

In the United States, an average of four or more individuals are wounded or killed in a single, violent event every day. A single event.

Pray that event is not in your neighborhood. But it might be. Don't be unprepared because you don't want to face the truth: we have an enemy who wants to kill everything we know to be good and true about the Master's vision.

Orange signifies an awareness of a real, potential threat. Your heart rate is elevated, and it should be. You've got enough awareness and enough training to recognize that something is not right. There is a guy who is definitely tweaking on drugs in the home and garden section of your local grocery store. There is a gun in that guy's pants. That certainly sounded like a scream for help or an explosion.

Not only do we need to be capable of recognizing things that are out of the ordinary (condition yellow), we need to be able to identify which of those things are immediate hazards and which are secondary.

In psychology, there is a term called the "bystander effect." It is an interesting phenomenon that started getting some attention after a particular event that happened in New York: the murder of Kitty Genovese. This young woman was brutally murdered—stabbed to death—in front of her apartment building. Reports vary on how many people witnessed the incident, but the most reputable reports put the number at around forty. Forty people witnessed the incident, marinating in condition orange. But what did they do next?

Red is the condition of acting once you've become aware of a threat. It is a simple condition, really, as it is characterized by being in action. The part that is difficult is the transition, mental and physical, from condition orange to condition red.

Do you know how many of those forty people called the police while Kitty Genovese screamed for help? How many got involved? How many helped in any fashion?

Zero.

The bystander effect is the psychological diffusion of responsibility among a crowd. In other words, everyone figures that someone else will do something about it.

In this case, no one did anything and a young woman died.

I would much rather have the regret of acting and wishing I hadn't, then NOT acting and wishing I had. We must be able to flick the mental switch and actually *do* something. Anything. That is why condition orange has its own color code, separate from red. It is a transition stage, but one that is hard to move out of.

I love the movie *The Incredibles*. Not only is it just an all-around fun movie, I love some of Mr. Incredible's tactics. As a superhero, he learns the hard way just how important it is to be prepared, aware, and fully alive. But when things are about to get messy, he knows how to flick the switch and go into action mode. If you've seen the movie, perhaps you've noticed that he says the same thing before almost every action scene:

"Showtime."

In tactical training, we call this a verbal mantra. A verbal mantra is a saying that helps connect (and sometimes isolate) the mental, spiritual, and physical elements of your body, telling each element that it's time to act in the way that you've trained it to.

It's showtime.

Making the jump from condition orange to condition red can be difficult without a mantra. Are you sure it's time to act? Most of the time the lines aren't very clear. When they are, use your mantra. Kick yourself into gear.

One verbal mantra my wife and I use to help us transition from orange to red is, "Go get the pickles." The reality is, I hate pickles. I would never tell anyone to go get pickles! So, when my wife hears me say this, she knows danger is close. She knows I'm in condition orange and will soon be in condition red.

What's more, she knows who I am. Sure, she knows her part because we have a plan: grab the kids, leave everything, get out the back, and scatter. (For those of you that don't know this strategy and are still practicing "lockdown," movement is life. MOVE!) But she also knows that, chances are, I won't be there with her. The vision the Master has laid upon my heart, a vision which has been refined by fire, is that of a guardian. A protector who can show the care and love of the Master even to those who don't deserve it. If I'm willing to live out that belief, you better believe I'm willing to die for it.

If you've ever thought about starting a violent event in public, you better pray to whatever master you serve that I'm not there when you do. Or stay in the pickle aisle.

Once you are in "showtime" mode, or condition red, it is very easy to lose control of your body. I'm sure you've heard of "fight or flight." This happens when you skip through condition red and end up in the final condition: Code **Black** .

In Code Black, your body starts doing things you don't want it to. You actually lose control, physically, mentally, and spiritually. That is no good at all.

Code Black is a direct descendent of unpreparedness. If you are unaware—in condition white—when a critical event takes place, chances are good that you'll be riding the rollercoaster all the way to Code Black. If you are untrained, guess what? Code

Black is right around the next corner. If you are not spiritually and mentally prepared and in line with the Master's vision? You guessed it—Code Black is all the more likely.

I feel bad for many of the police officers (and the civilians, for that matter) who I see on the news using excessive force. I can empathize with them, because I know where many of them are: they are in Code Black. I can see it in their eyes and hear it in their high and rapid tone of voice. They may not even realize that they are still using force, or that the amount of force they are using is way more than what is necessary.

When you start acting, you have to stay in control. You have to be so confident in your identity, even in the face of death, that you can love your enemy. This is a key element of a warrior who is in line with the Master's vision, and it is something that most warriors don't have.

I always find irony in the fact that a largely subjective world expects their guardians and protectors to be able to execute perfect, objective truth under stress.

It all starts with knowing your own identity and the Master's vision so confidently that you can never be shaken. Not even when there is a gun in your face, or when someone comes up and slaps your wife. I know, these are nerve-rattling, blood-boiling things. They both require immediate action. But they also both require you to be able to stay YOU.

The hulk is a funny movie character. He is NOT a funny or respectable reality. Flying off the handle means more people get hurt, there is more mental trauma, and there might even be jailtime... for you. Don't lose yourself in the heat of combat. It's easy to do, but it's a difficult journey back.

When you decide it's a good time to move from condition orange to condition red, you need to know how much force to use.

Well, how much *can* we use? Again, we've got to come back to our identity. Remember the vision of the Master. Your goal is not revenge or punishment. It's not to hurt anyone, though that may be necessary to protect others. The goal is to stop the enemy from destroying what you know to be objectively good and beautiful.

But before we continue our discussion about tactical force, we need to hit the pause button so that I can tell you about the 97/3 rule. The 97/3 rule is simple: 97% of the time, you should NOT need to use PHYSICAL FORCE to control a situation. Stop lifting weights 97% percent of the time and start practicing empathy in your communication. Work on your prayer life. Being strong is good, don't get me wrong. It's part of being prepared for the worst. But most of the time, good nonverbal and verbal communication will do the trick. What does this mean? It means using your team. Calling 911. Setting enforceable limits. Keeping your head. Loving others even when they don't deserve it, or they're messy, or they called your mamma a not-very-nice name. These things are key to de-escalation.

It is very, very difficult to pick a fight with someone who is loving, kind, and respectful, even in the worst moments. So that is the kind of warrior you want to be.

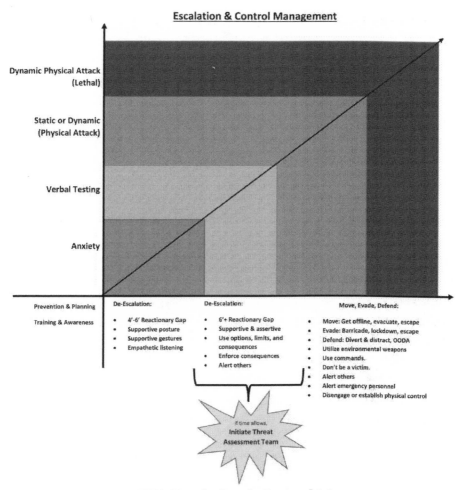

Image 5. TTA Escalation & Control Management

I remember when I re-opened our public defensive tactics training outreach center in Snohomish. We had been running free classes and gyms for several years with the idea of building mentorships with youth through defensive tactics training. It's a great, healthy way to mentor and speak truth into the body, mind, and spirit all at once. There aren't too many places where one can do that.

We were hosting classes in a church right off the main drag. It was Thursday night. I was setting up class with my instructor,

Dan, when a guy on his way to the bar walked right up to the front steps. I'm not quite sure what drew him in. He obviously saw us setting things up. He peered at us through the open church door and said something about "church queers" just loud enough for us to hear. He turned away like he had just done something heroic and the case was closed.

What he didn't expect was for me to call out to him. But I did. In fact, I invited him to come in and see what we were all about. The guy turned around and actually registered what we were doing. His eyes scanned over our wrestling mats, the five or six heavy bags laying on the floor, and the stacks of mouthguards and open-handed gloves laying about.

I tossed him a pair.

"How would you like a chance to increase your honor?" I asked him.

The guy turned around and ran out of there like I had dumped a bunch of hot coals on his head.

I've been in similar situations when the other person has not run away. They've stayed and gloved up, eager to prove their point. In each and every instance that the person has taken this first step, they've stayed for the entire training class and thanked me at the end. Hopefully, they learned that genuine love and humility are more powerful tools than the ability to use physical force.

Most people who want to pick a fight are looking for power and strength because they can't find any inside themselves. They are looking for the Master's vision, but when they come across someone who is actually living into that vision, they feel intimidated. And they should.

Ninety-seven percent of the time, physical force will not be and should not be necessary. And it should not be something we look for. We should not be known as men and women of violence. We should be known as peacekeepers. Guardians. Good stewards of objective truth. Kind, empathetic, and resourceful, even when it is hard.

But 3% of the time, de-escalation and prevention won't be enough.

Three percent of the time, you will have to decide to get involved physically or watch the enemy destroy and kill what you know and love. When the 3% day comes, you are going to have to be able to act with confidence, and quickly.

This 3% is very difficult for some individuals to grasp. I understand why. Violence between human beings is utterly traumatic and it's easier to pretend that you can avoid it 100% of the time.

When people are frightened of irrational things, we call it a phobia. If someone is scared of confined spaces, heights, or airplanes, we consider it a deviation from the typical human condition. But all of us consider the fear of close, interpersonal violence to be entirely normal.

Traumatic events come in many shapes and sizes: hurricanes, earthquakes, flooding, fire... just to name a few. All of these events threaten us. Most of them elicit a healthy level of fear and apprehension, and each of them can absolutely trigger PTSD. But none of them come close to causing the level of fear that most people experience from interpersonal violence. This is probably why the American Psychiatric Association states that PTSD may be especially severe or long lasting when it stems from a "human design."

Acting during the 3% moments is so difficult, in fact, that some folks have tried side-stepping the problem entirely through pacifism. Now, I must acknowledge some of the amazing role models of pacifism, who I greatly respect: Martin Luther King, Jr. and Gandhi are perhaps the two greatest figures at the forefront of any discussion about pacifism.

These individuals had the mental and spiritual awareness to recognize that, in their 3% situations, physical violence was not the correct response to accomplish their goals. They also knew, without any doubt, the vision that the Master had placed within them. They could see the objective truth.

However, these two servant-leaders faced an entirely different kind of 3% situation than what we are discussing here. Martin Luther King, Jr. and Gandhi both faced ongoing oppression. It was the minds of the people that needed to be changed. If history has shown us anything, it is that truth is not won through violence. It is won through belief, faith, and the power of words.

But in the 3% situation we're talking about here, minds can't be changed. When you are attacked by a bear, nonviolent de-escalation does not help you defend your position. It simply ensures that you will be mauled. The conversation about nonviolence is a good one, but it assumes that all men in all situations are able to be overpowered by unconditional love.

I do not contest that unconditional love is the most powerful force in the seen and unseen worlds. It is a characteristic distinct to humankind, stemming from the unique likeness we have to the Master. But the giving of unconditional love is not the right strategy in all situations.

Just a few weeks ago, another student was shot and killed in my state during a school shooting. The attacker returned from a suspension with a duffle bag carrying a semi-automatic rifle and a handgun. After the guns were deployed, the attacker's rifle jammed. At that point, a brave young student approached the attacker, who he knew, to try to talk him down. That young man became a victim.

On the 3% day, verbal de-escalation is not effective. It's time to act with force and aggression.

Pacifism makes two assumptions: it assumes that our opponent is NOT a bear or a pack of wolves, and it assumes that force cannot be used without depreciating ourselves into an ungodly state. This begs the question: can a man demean himself, enslaving himself to an evil master, to such a degree that he ceases to be human? Can the image of the master within our souls be corrupted to such an extent that it does not just reflect darkness, it festers like a petri dish until there is nothing left of the original vision? Does mankind have the power to destroy the vision of the Master?

The hard, clear answer is yes. A person enslaved to methamphetamine once said, "When I'm on meth, I am a monster." I have listened in on and conducted interviews with serial killers and serial rapists, and I have witnessed some of man's darkest facets. Some people truly are monsters.

Can the Master redeem the darkest soul? That depends on who you think the Master is. But if your master is a supernatural master that loves and cares for creation, then the answer is yes. Can the enemy destroy the Master's vision within us until there is no return? As we see through the eyes of the enemy himself, as well as through the countless acts of horror in the world, the answer is also yes.

The Master has given us the freedom *not* to choose him, even unto the point of utter self-destruction.

On the 3% kind of day, you might be facing naught but a shell of the Master's vision. Even worse, you might be facing the antithesis of the vision.

Surely all predatory behavior stems from a traumatized past. But in the moment when a predator attacks, I am not the judge. I am not the executioner. I am not a counselor. I am a guardian of what is right and good.

Understand that force is not necessarily animal-like violence, just like pacifism is not necessarily doing nothing. Pacifism and force can both be used to no good end. The one can be used as an excuse to do nothing, the other to act excessively. But in the right context, in the right situation, both can be used effectively and with the power of love. They each take discipline, understanding, and dedication to the master vision.

When the time comes to fight that bear and defend my loved ones, I will. And you can be certain I won't mince words about it beforehand.

I firmly believe that while we should be willing to fight for what we believe in, we should not be known as men and women of violence.

In fact, I have a real problem with UFC and MMA fighting. When I was in college and didn't have as much training, I toyed with the idea of amateur fighting. I had a buddy who was into it, and he took me to his training gym one night in an attempt to fuel my interest.

Long story short, I ended up sparring with one of their regular competitors. He was pretty decent. But after I knocked him a few good ones, he stopped training and started fighting. Before that fight was over, I had ruptured both of his eardrums. I learned a very valuable lesson that night: no one ever wins a fight.

To this day, that concept has remained true and I often go back to it. The only time a fight is worth having is when something disastrous needs to stop *right now*. I appreciate combat training events, don't get me wrong. I respect the fighters and the challenge of direct competition. But the problem with events like UFC is that they commercialize pain, not unlike the gladiator arenas of ancient Rome. They make battle a consumer ideal that can be sold on your TV.

The commercialization of pain has nothing to do with the vision the Master has laid upon our hearts. I cannot justify using such fierce tactics—mentally, spiritually, or physically— against another person merely for entertainment, money, and fame. Those things are not my Master.

Does physical training create amazing pathways for speaking to the spirituality and mentality of humans? Absolutely. Does it clarify the reality of the world, the effects of the enemy, and the vision of the Master? It does. But in these cases, we are talking about physical training and preparedness, not fighting.

The 97/3 rule is key to understanding how ineffective violent, physical force is for doing anything other than immediately stopping wrongdoing.

Words, love, and faith are much more powerful tools, with longer effectiveness. Unequivocally, they are more powerful than physical force. But they don't eliminate the need for the sword. They simply define the hands that hold it.

We must be confident enough in the vision of the Master to be able to see when physical action is needed and when it is not. I'll say this again: I would rather ACT and wish I hadn't, then do nothing and wish later that I had had the training or the courage to have done something. In the vast majority of 3% situations you or I will face, we will require immediate action to protect ourselves and others around us.

To tie this conversation into the real world, you should know that the 3% moment has a name in our legal system: justifiable use of force. Our legal system has almost unanimously determined that to be considered a justifiable use of force, an action must be the following two things:

1) <u>Reasonable</u>: another person, with similar training and experience facing a similar circumstance, would act in a similar way.

2) <u>Necessary</u>: no reasonable alternative appears to exist and the amount of force used is reasonable to effect the lawful purpose intended.

You'll notice that our legal system does its absolute best to base ancient, moral objective truths on subjective principles like "what another person would do." That's a tricky balance.

Chapter Six

Combative Training

This discussion has, so far, revolved around preparedness and awareness in our hearts and minds. We have talked very little about action.

As a combat training instructor, people ask me a lot of questions. What is the best martial arts? Which element should I learn first to be most effective in real-life situations? Boxing? Ju-Jitsu? Krav? Muay Thai?

The answer to all of these questions is the same: when the 3% kind of day happens, the bad guy will always have the jump on you, regardless of your training. That is the bummer of real life. It's not at all like your boxing gym. You don't get to be wearing your wrestling shoes. Your hands are not going to be wrapped up.

We are response oriented. The bad guys always act first. We have to try to catch up. This means that regardless of what techniques you know, you must be confident in the Master's vision above all else. Remember the story of how Jon Meis took down the active shooter at Seattle Pacific University? Learn *that* form of martial arts. It's called faith.

Once you have that, then you can move onto the easier elements of training.

In any given encounter, your opponent wants something. It is important for us to identify what it is. We need to know as much about our opponent as possible to defeat him (or her), *especially* regarding their motivating force. What spiritual and mental state are they in? What physical elements are they after, if any? Most likely, you will be able to generate answers to these questions relatively quickly using situational awareness.

Generally, there are three fluid levels of objectives for which people are willing to assault someone else: material things, bodily pleasure, and life destruction. Simply put, in a violent, 3% situation, the aggressor is after something you have, they want to hurt you because it makes them feel good, or they simply want to kill you.

The reasons motivating each level of an aggressor's actions vary.

Sometimes their actions are based on desperation. Sometimes they are based on the desire to carry out the enemy's will to destroy what is good. Assume that if your opponent is acting, they have already justified in their minds the pain they are causing you. They might realize later that their justification was wrong. Or they may feel guilty and think about what master in their lives caused them to cause hurt. They may even turn the corner and give up their fake master for a new one.

But in the heat of attack, your response remains the same. It will be whatever you've trained yourself to do.

Our physical response *should* be entirely based upon the level of objective our enemy has. Most people, even police officers, don't have enough training to recognize what that objective is and to act accordingly in the moment. However, there are some key observations that can help us determine an opponent's objective quickly, based on their actions and the weapon system they are using. I'll give you an example.

What would you do if you were walking to your car after going shopping, and some guy jumps out from behind a bush? He is bigger than you. He is butt-naked and unarmed. You are unprepared (meaning also unarmed). What do you do?

Well, you have a split second to identify what this guy is after. You can tell some things right off the bat: you're in a supermarket parking lot, for example. This would be an entirely different situation if you were outside of a nudist club. You can also tell that the aggressor is not in a correct mental state. He's naked (and there is no nudist club in sight). That observation is big. You can probably gauge his size, access to weapons, and physical ability with some level of accuracy. But don't ever give an aggressor the benefit of the doubt. I always assume a threat is after my life until they prove otherwise.

They might prove otherwise by saying something like, "Give me your groceries!" Okay, great. Now I've got some context. But what if this person said, "Get in the car and drive: we're going to my place." Whoa. Now we're going somewhere else entirely.

Either way, I have to know what this guy wants.

In a situation like this, there are many dynamic variables. So, we must create a model for our action-reaction system because we'll never be able to accurately predict every variable in every possible situation.

Fortunately, every human being processes information in the same way. And it is very powerful to know how this processing works, both for you and for the violator.

The model for how our processing works is called the OODA loop, and it is a tactical way of expressing how humans react to their environment in the context of time.

OODA-LOOP

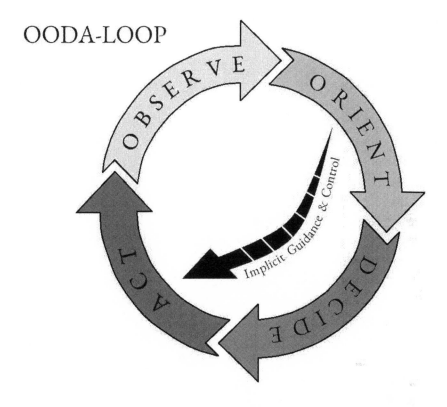

Image 6. The OODA Loop

Observe.
Orient.
Decide.
Act.
RE-observe the changes.
RE-orient.
RE-decide.
So on and so forth.

Each step in the OODA loop is key. Even more important is the time it takes for the OODA loop to operate.

You need to understand that *everyone* goes through the OODA loop, whether they like it or not. This includes both you AND whoever the aggressor is. The principle here is that this loop affects you both. So, if you can control the OODA loop, you suddenly become a Jedi Master.

When I train OODA loop tactics, I literally call them "Jedi mind tricks." Because they are. They're crazy. If you still don't believe that these spiritual, mental energy tactics are deeply interconnected with our physical ones, take a break and go expand your mind. You are not living in a reality that is consistent with the facts of the world.

A master in OODA loop tactics can change your focus, slow your mental processing time, and act before you can even guess what they are about to do. We are going to talk about the stages of the OODA loop and I'll deliver some key tactical takeaways for each of them.

Observe:

In a split second, we need to be able to observe where we are, who is around us, and what our options are. Observing takes practice, but some key things to focus on are "pre-attack indicators."

These are small physical indicators that betray what the mind is thinking and what the body is about to do. Like clues in an investigation, enough pre-attack indicators grouped together can indicate what your opponent is about to do, sometimes even before they are aware of it themselves.

Pre-attack indicators can present immediately or show themselves slowly over time. A single indicator by itself does not prove much of anything. But with enough indicators grouped together, you can get a pretty good view of what is happening on the inside, especially if something is wrong.

When discussing indicators, it is important to remember the theory of escalation: people typically do not just snap. There are indicators of violence, and they often predictively get worse and worse the longer the situation goes on. Aggression escalates through three different stages: first there are nonverbal indicators in the "anxiety stage," then there are verbal indicators in the "testing stage," and lastly there is physical violence in the "attack stage."

Each violent stage and its indicators suggest what specific response we should take. With anxiety, our best response is to provide support and empathy, encouragement and counseling. In the testing stage, the violator is typically seeing where the line is. Setting enforceable limits and boundaries can be a key technique for de-escalation. When you reach the attack stage (which is less than 3% of the time, remember), we need to act. Now.

Here is a short list of general indicators that are worth being aware of:

Unsolicited comments about violence. Sudden lack of hygiene. Vague complaints or threats. Emotionally unstable responses. Explosive outbursts without provocation. Increase in alcohol consumption or drug use. Sudden withdrawal from friends or decreased social ability. Actions or comments that indicate a perceived loss of power and a desire to regain control through extreme measures.

It is common to display some of these things during rough times in our lives. Like many people, I tend to pull away from those I love when I'm hurting. Indicators like those listed above show us that something is wrong. Deep inside, the vision of the Master is not being met, or it is being drowned out, or maybe it is even being strangled out by the enemy. These indicators are worth noting and they require intervention. Support those folks and let them know they are not alone.

Isolation, rejection, or shunning is never the correct response when observing these indicators unless you are in danger yourself. We should be loving even in the worst moments, but not to the point of becoming a slave to a false master. If you feel like you recognize violent indicators from someone you know but don't feel capable of acting on them, call emergency services.

It's never a bad time to call for aid. No one automatically gets arrested when you call 911 or the non-emergency number. Your local first responders can be a great resource for support and for help. That is the idea of using your team. Involve more resources. Get some help in there.

If you're not comfortable calling 911 for whatever reason, call my office (1-425-773-2930). I promise you that I will do all I can to help you walk through the situation you are facing.

Other pre-attack indicators can be more immediate and require instantaneous recognition and action:

Invasion of the reactionary gap.

This is the most important, immediate pre-attack indicator. The reactionary gap (or, reaction gap) is a term used to describe the amount of space you need around you to be able to react (OODA) to your environment. When someone gets within your reaction gap, they can act before you can react. A typical reactionary gap distance is anywhere from 3-25 feet, depending on what side of the body we're discussing and what weapon system the violator is operating.

In short, most physical attacks will happen after the violator closes the distance between you. If someone is getting close to you in a threatening situation, you should maintain distance and have some serious red flags going off.

Reaching with the hands.

The deadliest weapons are manipulated by the human hand. Knives, firearms, baseball bats, hammers—all held and manipulated in the hand. If you are in a potentially violent situation and you are not watching the aggressor's hands, you are way behind the curve. If you are watching their hands and their hands suddenly disappear behind their back, between their car seats, or into their jacket, you should be wondering what they are reaching for. You should not assume it is a handkerchief.

Be aware of how concealed weapons look on the human body and in unknown spaces, like vehicles. My wife and I always play a game when we are in public of seeing who can spot the most concealed weapons. Weapons tend to be heavy, with jagged edges and contour lines. Those lines are visible through light clothing.

The human mind is also very aware of weapons, especially firearms, which affects a person's movement. It is very typical for someone carrying a firearm to have an unusual gait, like holding the firearm with one hand to support it while running through the rain. Most people will also unconsciously fidget with their weapon, absentmindedly touching it to reassure themselves it is still there.

Shift in weight/settling of the body.

The center mass of an individual is the first thing that moves in an attack (outside of the hands). If the hips or chest suddenly turn, twist, or settle, it is an immediate indication that the rest of the body is about to spring into action, typically with a strike or kick.

Target glance.

The aggressor is going to be OODA looping, just like you. They will be observing and orienting themselves to you, especially if you have a potential weapon handy. A target glance is when the aggressor quickly looks at your weapon or the area on your body that he is about to strike. This "sneak peek" can be quite obvious, and it is typically a precursor or part of the decision-making pause.

Decision-making pause.

Each portion of the OODA loop takes time. Typically, when an aggressor is transitioning from an anxiety or testing stage to the attack stage, they pause for a brief moment. This is their brain completing the OODA loop and deciding which violent action is best for them to take. After the decision-making pause, the violator will be in the "act" phase of the OODA loop and will execute their decided action. Like a sudden, violent strike.

At a mental health training course, I once had an officer tell me a fantastic story about the decision-making pause. Just a few weeks earlier, he had been called to escort a threatening patient to another wing in a hospital. This patient had a record of violent outbursts. Yet this officer decided to escort the patient up to the second floor alone. In an elevator.

Hear any warning bells going off?

Initially, the patient was in the testing stage, being quite verbally aggressive. Then, in the middle of the elevator ride, the patient suddenly grew very quiet. The officer remembered the patient looking at him very hard, face growing pale.

This happened because the blood was moving away from the patient's face and into his core muscles. With which he was about to try to kill this officer. A few short moments later, the patient lunged at the officer, desperately trying to bite his jugular.

Afterward, this officer was very excited to receive some quality training.

Preparing for violence.

When someone starts taking off rings and jewelry, setting aside valuable items, stretching, making bombs, or gathering weapons, they are getting ready for something. If these actions are paired with other pre-attack indicators or threats of violence, you can be sure that things are about to heat up.

Observation and awareness are the start of everything. But physical indicators are not everything. When the hair on the back of your next starts to rise, or you feel deep in your bones that something is wrong, something probably is. Don't ignore these things.

Even if something is not visibly wrong in your immediate,

physical vicinity, there may be something bigger happening. Remember, the foundation of our vision assumes that we are threatened spiritually and mentally, possibly even more so than we are physically. When you feel in your heart that something is amiss, be aware of your surroundings and be a warrior in prayer.

Orient:

Once we observe what is going on, we must orient ourselves to the threat. This orientation encompasses knowing where you are in relation to your surroundings. Are you in a parking lot? The back room? An aisle at the shopping center? At home? This overall orientation will help you to approach or flee the situation tactically. It will help you stay out of unnecessary danger (like walking in front of a car), and it will help you use the element of surprise to your advantage.

Of course, you should already know where you are. But a key part of your orientation is knowing exactly where your escape routes are and where the nearest form of communication is. Where is the nearest door and window? How can you get out of them quickly? Where is the nearest help? Is it a sharp yell, a short run, or a phone call away?

This defensive thought process should include identifying cover and concealment. Cover includes any object that can stop a bullet from a firearm. Some examples would be a concreate foundation, a filing cabinet full of papers, an engine block, or a big tree. Concealment is something that will hide you visually from a violent aggressor, like getting low and hiding behind your desk or couch, or hunkering down in your car.

We also need to be thinking offensively. A key mistake I consistently see during lockdown drills is that individuals hide behind concealment without preparing themselves for the worst-case scenario. They huddle together, unarmed. This is why active shooters' hit rate is around 90%. They tend to shoot easy batches of targets. Instead, look for your nearest environmental weapon. What is nearby that you can use to disrupt your violator's OODA loop? What can you use to disrupt their vision and overwhelm their senses? A fire-extinguisher, a chair, or a tire iron are all good things to have handy.

Of course, you can never tell how many threats there really are. When I host drills and exercises with law enforcement, I love throwing in what is called a "secondary threat." It is always the non-obvious threat that isn't thought about until it is too late.

We always have to be looking for the second threat. Eyes up! Scan and assess.

We also need to orient ourselves toward help and escape. Statistically speaking, the first person who starts thinking outside of the box during a violent event is going to win. How can you escape? What do you have available?

By itself, your body has many natural offensive and defensive tools. Orient those tools to your advantage. Use them to get on top of the OODA loop.

Decide:

Once you've observed and oriented, you must decide what you are going to do. Ask yourself, what is the aggressor's objective? What is *your* objective? Typically, your objective is going to be to stop the violent action or to merely survive. You have to weigh the scales, determining what level of incident you are facing and what you are capable of safely executing. Decide what is best for you and the others around you.

Remember, during a crisis situation, most other individuals are going to be borderline Code Black. It is likely that they will follow your lead if you encourage them verbally and lead by example. The more training, the more practice, and the more pre-planning you have undertaken, the less time the decision-making process will take.

Act:

Do what you just decided to do. Move, evade, or defend. Use your mantra. It's go-time. Pickle time. Showtime. Do it. Act with sudden surprise and aggression. Act with speed and confidence. The attacker is likely expecting a victim. Don't be one.

Re-observe:

I hate it in the movies when the good guy executes a great action, thinks he has won, but doesn't get his eyes up and looking around for the next threat. In real life, there is no victory dance. The music doesn't transition us into a new scene. In real life, every action changes the variables in the scene and makes it necessary to conduct another OODA loop process.

A fundamental tactic in close quarters battle (CQB) training is to be continually scanning your surroundings. Low to high. Front to back. Always be looking for the next threat. Don't assume your aggressor is alone. Too many people have made that mistake and then been taken by surprise by an attack from behind. They weren't looking for the next threat.

If there isn't another threat, there is always something left to do. Have you called 911 yet? Do you need to apply first aid? Do you need to encourage and support other victims by telling them the truth about the world and themselves? Always re-observe for what is next.

Observe. Orient. Decide. Act. Repeat.

There are several powerful takeaways in OODA loop training. One of the most fundamental is the importance of time.

Depending on the level of training you have, the OODA loop can take between .5 and 3 seconds to complete. Think about it: first we need to process our situation, then we must cognitively make sense of what we are seeing, and finally we need to send an electronic signal from our mind to our body, directing it to physically do something. Physiologically, this takes time. How much time it takes depends on the speed with which you can execute this equation:

Perceptual + Cognitive + Motor-processing time = Reaction time.

The more training and stress inoculation you have, the more implicit your mental guidance and physical control will be during this equation. In fact, training and preparedness can even short-circuit this loop, allowing your reaction time to consistently be faster than your opponent.

But there are other techniques that we can use to slow down our opponent's OODA loop.

What happens if, for example, what you are observing or processing changes right in the middle of your OODA loop process? Well, then you have to start the whole thing all over again.

This is the power of the OODA loop in any situation.

If an active shooter walks into your building, what is that attacker expecting to observe? A bunch of helpless victims. But what if, instead of finding everyone cowering on the floor like they expect, they walk into a dark room and smack into a hailstorm of chairs being thrown at their head?

I guarantee their OODA loop will reset. And, for a few moments, you will be in control. If you stay ahead of the OODA loop, you will survive.

My favorite drills in active shooter training are OODA loop drills. I'll share one of my favorites with you. It is a Krav-based drill in which a student is given a simple math equation to complete as fast as possible. The key is that their OODA loop is being continually reset while they're doing the math, typically by having tennis balls thrown at them. Before the scene starts, I will duct-tape a stuffed animal lion onto my head and arm myself to the teeth, wielding a large training gun and a baseball bat... just to see if they notice the obvious secondary threat while having tennis balls thrown at them in the middle of doing a math problem.

Can you imagine trying to do a simple math equation while people are throwing tennis balls at you? It can be frustrating. Not only does this give everyone in training a chance to see how the mental process is slowed down when you upset the OODA loop (in this case by throwing things), it shows the beginning stages of Code Black as the heart rate increases. Tunnel vision and an extreme loss of critical-thinking ability are key facets of what is experienced during this exercise.

To this day, I have yet to do a training where an individual in the math scene has recognized that I have a fake lion taped to my head and am holding a gun in one hand and a baseball bat in the other. Yet I've been walking around them the entire time, yelling and waving the weapons in their face.

Meanwhile, the rest of the class watches in shock as the student participating in the scene remains oblivious. Not even one participant has ever realized that their instructor just went crazy. They are focused on the math and the tennis balls. By default, their OODA loop is entirely under my control. They don't remember it. They don't see it.

Amazing. Jedi mind tricks.

Understanding the OODA loop is key to whatever form of combatives you train in. Knowing OODA loop principles are by themselves "the best martial art." However, I'll give you my two cents on which combative forms are better than the next, so you can invest your time, money, and resources in the right places.

But first, let's clear up some terminology. "Combatives" is the big-picture term that refers to the forms and methodologies that prepare an individual for a use-of-force encounter. It is not combat itself, which is the actual engagement of the enemy, but it encompasses all the physical strategies that professional training prepares you to *use* in combat. CQB, handgun, hand-to-hand—these are all combative forms. These are the elements of combat training that help you prepare for a 3%

confrontation.

Now, without any doubt, the best strategy in a 3% confrontation is to have a superior weapon. Real-life, threatening encounters don't happen in controlled environments. It'll be dark and cold. It'll be three vs. one, and you'll be the one. One of your attackers will have a knife, a stick, or brass knuckles. Or they all will.

There are always variables, and those variables are only equalized by a superior weapon. Your body can be a weapon, no doubt about it. But regardless of how much training you have, lethal-force tools like knives and firearms close out fights very quickly.

For the real-life 3% kind of day, the number-one strategy for survival is to learn how to carry, protect, and use a firearm. And then do so. If you take preparedness seriously, guns have to be on the menu. The reason is simple: bad guys have lethal-force tools and they are not afraid to use them. And they *will* use them, no matter how many laws we have in place. Which makes sense. If they don't care about the objective vision, it's a good bet they don't care about subjective laws.

Four years ago, the Bureau of Alcohol, Tobacco, Firearms and Explosives described the availability of illegal guns on the black market as, "so readily available the price on the black-market is just a few hundred higher than retail". With increased use of dark and deep-net web use, the truth is simple: individuals who are determined to get weapons can do so.

Here is where it all ties together: most aggressors we are talking about here are not "reactive". They are "planners".

If I install a metal detector and an 8-foot barbed wire fence around a school, what are the bad guys going to start planning for? A metal detector. And a barbed-wire fence. Will they be able to defeat those security measures if they really want to? They absolutely will. We have seen it time and time again.

Crime prevention through environmental design is important. Legislation and gun laws are important. They influence violence in our neighborhoods. But neither are quick-fix solutions to the problem of violence.

If bad guys have a lethal force tool and you don't, your bad day just got worse.

Don't think that the good guys with guns, training, and badges are going to be there to help you when the crisis situation happens. Most of the time, they are at least eight minutes away. On a 3% kind of day, that is an eternity. You're going to be on your own. But if you have some quality training, you can make it.

Not surprisingly, carrying a firearm (or any other lethal-force object) requires the most training out of all the available martial arts forms. Unlike other martial arts, which you can manipulate without a 100% knowledge of the subject, firearms have no room for error.

During the time I was in law enforcement, I remember hearing about an incident involving an off-duty police officer who was conceal carrying a firearm when he stopped by a McDonald's. Unbeknownst to him, it was about to turn into a 3% kind of day.

While waiting in line, he realized that the McDonald's was getting robbed. A man was brandishing a semi-automatic gun and demanding cash from the restaurant manager.

Do you remember your training? First, we have to be aware of the incident. Check. Then we have to recognize what our violator wants in less than a split second.

What does this bad guy want? I should think money. How much? Well, how much do you think is in a McDonald's? Not very much. In this case, there wasn't more than a few hundred dollars up for grabs.

Long story short, this police officer drew down on the guy and ended up getting into a gunfight. Yes, he killed the bad guy. But that's not actually the end. Because bullets don't stop when they hit something, and bullets shot at you don't vanish into thin air when they miss.

This is one of the most fundamental rules of firearms training: know your target, your backstop, *and what is around you.*

During the gunfight, a bullet from the bad guy's gun struck a 9-year-old girl in the head. She died instantly.

It's easy to evaluate an incident afterwards and point out everything that went wrong. It's easy to point to broad, overarching principles when things go bad, like saying "guns shouldn't be in public places." Humans always tend to take the easier road when faced with an obstacle.

The reality is, incidents unfold more rapidly than you can think. So if you don't have the necessary training, you are always behind. The incident at the McDonald's started off just like any other day. But our days can quickly change. If you don't have training, you are not going to be of any help on a 3% kind of day. You'll actually make the problem worse. Regardless of whether you have a firearm or not.

Long after the incident, I read a great article by that police officer. He wrote about how he snapped into "cop mode" in the McDonald's without taking the totality of his circumstances into account. Understand, police officers are required to go through thousands of hours of training, and the vast majority of that training focuses on the use of force and how to use a firearm. They receive professional training on getting involved. Nonetheless, this police officer had never realistically prepared for this very specific kind of event, one where he *wasn't in uniform.* There was a gap in his training.

My point here is that while carrying a gun is, without any doubt, the most effective solution to the 3% reality, carrying a gun requires extensive training. When I say extensive training, I mean extensive training for realistic scenarios. If you don't have this training, you shouldn't be carrying a gun. Because you'll make things worse. Not better.

You need to be able to act correctly without thinking. You must be able to identify cover and concealment, know your target and beyond, and recognize the hazards around you, all in a fraction of an instant. You have to prioritize all of this information and make a decision. You need to be able to move, think, and react, all while staying off your trigger and keeping your gun pointed in a safe direction. You need to manipulate your firearm and your opponent, and you need to be able to use OODA principles instead of tunneling your vision in on either your gun or your opponent's. Sometimes all of this will add up to not using physical force. And sometimes it will mean you don't get involved at all.

That's just a basic, basic, start. You'll notice that, in this section, I'm not talking about things like the fundamentals of marksmanship, retention training, or ballistic responsibility when carrying a handgun. In this conversation, I'm assuming that you are already a master at those things. If not, you shouldn't be carrying.

You can't get this level of training by shooting at your static range. You can't get it by attending a three-day course or even a three-month course.

The vast majority of gun owners who end up getting shot during a 3% encounter get shot with their own firearm. That is because it's relatively easy to own a gun and it is NOT at all easy to get the necessary training on how to use one correctly in combat.

So, am I proponent of you carrying a firearm? It depends. What is your vision from the Master? Are you carrying a firearm for your ego or for the truth? Are you ready to carry it concealed all the time, which is both uncomfortable and a huge responsibility? How confident are you with your training? Can you hit a bad guy and recognize how many walls your bullet will travel through before fragmenting enough to become non-lethal? Are you a good enough marksman to hit a moving aggressor without hitting any of the countless scared victims who are running in front, behind, to the side, and possibly above your target? Would you be able to retain your firearm when a trained aggressor is trying to take it from you? Do you know when to back down and when to put up a fight?

These are hard questions, and some of them are impossible to answer unless you are walking with the Master and his vision.

If you have the vision and a level of training to be part of the solution, then I'm all for it. Personally, I know very few people who have both.

If you don't have both, you are going to be a worse problem than the initial one. Leave your gun locked up in your safe until you've invested in many long hours of quality tactics training and you've asked the hard questions about the world.

In a real fight, you are always looking to turn the odds in your favor. There are no rules, no lines of fairness, nothing off-limits. This is why Krav Maga is my second recommendation for individuals looking for quality, real-life training for the 3% kind of day.

Krav focuses on several key elements during a violent encounter, but awareness of environmental weapons is, without any doubt, my favorite. I see scuffles all the time in which a chair, a garbage-can lid, a pencil, or a sweatshirt were available and not used. But these items, when used correctly, can be lethal elements that turn the tide of a use-of-force encounter.

This must be why the *Jason Bourne* movie series is one of my favorites. I absolutely love their combative scenes because it's like watching a training video. There are many scenes that take place in urban environments. I recall seeing a book, a lamp, a washcloth, a newspaper, and a pencil all being used in a variety of ways during Bourne's fight scenes. In his hands, these items become OODA loop reset devices and weapons. That's what I am talking about!

The main principle of Krav, however, is neutralizing your opponent as quickly as possible. Krav facilitators are not at all shy. In fact, they require a careful study of the human body's weak and vulnerable areas. They teach students how to overwhelm those areas as quickly as possible. Krav also spends time building strength, speed, and aggression to accomplish the task at hand.

For these reasons, Krav is dangerous for those that do not have a vision from the Master. Having an art form that stimulates and encourages aggression without a platform of love, kindness, and humility is not a good thing. It is a very bad thing.

But, it is very important to understand aggression. What's more, it is important to be okay with it.

Most people think that aggression is an inherently bad thing. Aggression is a term used to describe the physical, mental, and spiritual state of an individual, typically when they are exhibiting violent tendencies.

Most people also think that hate is a bad thing. Hate is a term used to describe a feeling of utter resentment or loathing toward a particular thing or action. It usually leads to wishing that whatever brought about the feeling is completely destroyed.

I want to share an ancient proverb with you and point out a few learning principles. It is one of my favorites. It comes from a book of wisdom called Proverbs:

"There are six things the Lord hates, seven that are detestable to him: Haughty eyes. A lying tongue. Hands that shed innocent blood. Feet that are quick to rush into evil. A false witness who pours out lies. And a man who stirs up dissention among brothers."

First, I want you to realize that not only is this proverb suggesting that the Master detests some of our actions, he absolutely hates them. He wants them to be utterly destroyed.

The reality is, if you're serving a master that doesn't hate evil, there is a problem with your vision. If you serve a master that tolerates evil, you need to ask yourself what that means for your vision. This proverb depicts a master who wants to utterly destroy evil. That sounds a little aggressive. Because it is.

This is not an excuse to justify your massive ego, your bullying tendencies, or your negative behavior. The vast majority of the time (in fact, at least 97% of the time) aggression is not a healthy or accurate response. But 3% of the time, aggression may not only be good, it may very well be necessary.

The majority of human beings are not usually aggressive creatures. Even when cornered and threatened, a significant percentage of human beings will go into Code Black and their body systems will shut down. Fight or flight is not accurate. It is more accurately flight or freeze. Very, very rarely will "fight" be a natural survival response from a common, reasonable human in today's technology driven world.

This is good, because most of the time, when we are threatened, it is by an individual who is merely looking to instigate a reaction or response. That is the 97% kind of day.

The rest of the time, our non-aggressive freeze syndrome is not at all working in our favor for survival.

One great methodology taught in Krav is called the -5 to +10 principle. This principle dictates that when you or someone else is being attacked, the attacker expects to have the upper hand. On a scale of -10 to +10, they expect to be at a +5 as the aggressor. They expect you to be at a -5 as the victim. This gives them power to take whatever they want.

I hate it when strong people use their strength to take what is good and beautiful from those who are weaker than they. It is a righteous feeling and is usually followed by aggressive pre-attack indicators. From me.

Krav teaches us how to use this aggression to reset the violator's OODA loop. If they are expecting a -5 and instead suddenly find themselves facing a small brown bear at a +10, they fall behind the OODA loop curve. Now they are the victim. They are fighting to catch up. And many times, that OODA loop upset changes the entire tide of the confrontation.

I respect this outlook and find it very handy to teach others, especially when they do not have time to practice in-depth combatives. The reality is, most people just don't care enough about this topic to spend a dedicated amount of time and energy changing the way they think and react.

In our culture, we generally expect to see impactful results after trying something for about two minutes. If we don't see results, we aren't interested. Unfortunately, combatives don't work like that (which is why there aren't any pictures of techniques in this book). Hand-to-hand combatives require a substantial investment because they naturally require a total makeover of your mind, heart, and body.

Krav, however, can teach people very simple techniques that are based on aggression and require minimal practice and skill. When I only have eight hours in someone's life to teach them how to confidently defeat an active shooter, those principles come in handy.

My third and final recommendation is BJJ, or Brazilian jujitsu. BJJ fans claim that BJJ is "the best" tactical form of defense primarily because of their theory that "all fights end up on the ground." If that were true, I would agree. But it's not. Fights only end up on the ground if you lose your footing. To that end, avoiding going to the ground is a key principle of every combative martial arts form I teach, and avoiding being grounded really isn't that difficult if you are being mindful, have some training, and are using your environment (like swinging around a chair).

That being said, and in all fairness to BJJ, some 3% days *do* end up as a scuffle on the ground. While it is often simple enough to disengage and resume your Krav or other stand-up tactics, it is invaluable to know how to dominate on the ground.

When BJJ is combined with Krav ground survival, it is a very effective form of martial arts.

The thing I like about BJJ the most is the ability to submit my opponent without doing considerable damage to him or her. The joint manipulations, the choking tactics, and the various restraining positions taught in BJJ are invaluable, especially if I want to defeat my opponent through love. These tactics are called "control tactics," in contrast to defensive tactics, and they are absolutely worth knowing.

I want to invest in tactics training to such a degree that when the 3% day comes, I don't have to kill my opponent. I want to have enough skill and enough training that I can effectively defeat that individual *and* save their life in the same moment.

There will not be a single time, a greater chance, to speak into an aggressor's life than in the middle of the 3% day. Most of the time, they won't be listening until you are in control and the scene is over. But remember that most people lash out because of a problem: an old wound, a lack of respect, or the need for attention. They are looking for a full life, or once were.

The Master has a vision for everyone, and it is not beyond his ability to call someone into that vision under the might of *your* hand, in the heat of battle. Especially if you have enough training to be aware of your opponent's spiritual state and a desire to defeat him while being true to the Master.

Because BJJ is a martial art based on submission, it is much easier to learn an applicable, useful foundation in BJJ than it is to learn tactical weapon manipulations or Krav. There is less risk to your training partner and less risk of hurting yourself. It is also much more widespread, with a good dojo in almost every major city in the U.S. Good Krav trainers are rare, and good tactical-oriented firearms instructors are much rarer still.

Chapter Seven

The Violent Intruder

Imagine this: you're in your office or school doing your normal, everyday tasks. Suddenly you hear several gunshots from the hallway. A breathless co-worker runs in. She yells, "Someone is shooting!" Do you know what to do? If you've been through any active-shooter based training program, you have an idea of what to do.

Now imagine this: you're in the front office doing your normal, everyday duties. Suddenly, the door opens. An upset person marches in, demanding to speak to your boss. They are escalated, with face flushed and brows narrowed. And they are gripping a hammer in their hand.

Do you know what to do?

Very few people will answer this question correctly. Here are some common answers:

"I'd call 911."

"I'd try to calm the person down."

"I'd step between them and the entrance to the rest of the facility."

Would you do those same things if they were carrying a gun in their hand? Do you think this person is really there for a construction meeting?

Fifteen times more people are stabbed and beaten to death every year than are killed with rifles. Did you know that? If someone has put in the forethought and pre-planning to bring a weapon into the vicinity, you can bet they already have a plan to use it. They have already justified the behavior in their minds.

What kind of person is this person? An active shooter? An active killer? Or a violent intruder?

What exactly are we trying to prepare for when we offer training programs that teach us how to respond to violent incidents? Are we teaching people to respond to violence? Or are we conditioning people to only take action when guns are involved?

We have to start correcting our terminology (and even more importantly, our training) when we talk about violent incidents in the workplace. There are three common terms floating around and I want to address each of them before we wrap up our conversation on combative training.

Active Shooter:

This term is the most common. It is used by the FBI, who define it as "an individual actively engaged in killing or attempting to kill people in a confined and populated area."

But the active shooter terminology has a fundamental error. It teaches everyone that a gun must be involved when someone is trying to kill you. Moreover, the FBI's definition suggests that active shooters can only engage in confined areas: not on the road, in the parking lot, or at an open-air concert.

False.

Active Killer:

This term is used by many law enforcement agencies to counter the issue with the "active shooter" terminology. The idea is that a gun is NOT necessary in order for a violent incident to be synonymous with an "active shooter situation."

This term is much more accurate, but there is still a fundamental problem: this term assumes that *killing* is in progress. Does someone have to be in the very act of killing before we react appropriately? Do I have to be dying before acknowledging that my life is in danger? If you wait that long, it's going to be too late.

Violent Intruder:

This is any person who intrudes upon the area (ANY area) where you are and demonstrates an intent to do violence toward another person. It could involve a gun. It could involve a hammer. It could involve a car.

And what is the correct response?

Move. Evade. Defend.

Professional SWAT law enforcement teams have less than a 20% shoot-hit rate in real life. Active shooters have over a 90% shoot-hit rate. What's the difference?

The answer is simple: easy targets. Even from a close distance it is very, very difficult to hit a moving target with a firearm—even with advanced tactics training. It is very easy, however, to shoot someone huddled under a desk.

Wait, isn't it common practice during a lockdown to huddle together on the floor, under desks and in corners?

Yes.

See a problem?

Many people are not familiar with the history of "lockdown." Lockdowns were started in the 1980's within the Los Angeles County School District. They were called "Drive-by shooting drills." The drills were created in response to rampant gang activity in the area. Simply put, drive-by shootings were happening all the time and school staff wanted to be able to keep kids safe.

This new "lockdown" strategy caught nation-wide attention. Before anyone realized what was happening, "lockdowns" were suddenly considered the best response for ANY violent event—

whether they were happening on-campus or off. No research was conducted. No tests were completed.

You're a smart person. If you had a violent person at large in the community and the only thing known about their whereabouts was that they <u>weren't</u> at your school or workplace, what would be a good response? Lockdown. Of course. Keep the area you know to be safe secure. And stay there.

But what happens if you instigate that same policy and apply it to all violent events—even the ones where a known threat is located on your campus already? Lockdown doesn't seem like such a great idea anymore.

Unfortunately, the United States learned the hard way that lockdown just doesn't apply in all violent situations. Columbine. Sandy Hook. Virginia Tech. When a violent intruder is already on your campus or breaches your campus, lockdown is not just ineffective, it creates easy targets. It's like locking yourself in a closet with someone trying to kill you. It creates a mass-casualty event.

From 2000 to 2013, the FBI conducted a study of active shooter events within the United States. They analyzed lockdown as a response and, based on their results, the Department of Homeland Security released a new, nation-wide best-practice response to active shooter situations. They recommended it for schools, hospitals, houses of worship... anywhere an active shooter might strike.

They called this new, recommended program "Run. Hide. Fight."

Since 2013, the Run. Hide. Fight. program has gained a lot of awareness but very little traction within communities. This is because Run. Hide. Fight. is a fear-based response. I'll tell you what I mean.

If I ran into your classroom or workplace and yelled, "RUN!!!" what would you do? You would stop thinking and you would start running. Your body would commit a gross motor skill while your brain was left behind trying to catch up... and creating dysfunction along the way.

If I ran into your classroom or workplace and yelled, "HIDE!!!" or "FIGHT!!!" your response would be exactly the same: gross motor skill, no thinking, dysfunction, chaos, fear.

Is Run. Hide. Fight. better than a lockdown? Well, it depends how much brainpower you lose during the critical event. It certainly isn't more beneficial to run toward danger. And if you don't stop to identify stimulus in your environment before acting, that's just what might happen.

The key is, we cannot ever stop thinking during a crisis, especially a violent crisis, because of how rapidly things can change.

This is why the TTA's Move. Evade. Defend. approach is the most effective response to a violent intruder event.

<u>Move</u> is a statement that requires additional information: "where?" and "how?" are two questions that we need to answer before we run into trouble. Where is safe? Where is the danger located? How can I get away from it in the safest way possible?

<u>Evade</u> is a dynamic term, not a static "hide." Evade requires the individual to continually re-assess their surroundings—the changing environment—and make decisions. When you're being hunted, there are times to move. There are also times to be still and quiet, and there are times to barricade. There is no defined order or process... you have to act based on how the situation changes.

Finally, there are times to <u>Defend</u>. Fight implies aggression, speed, and a life-or-death attitude. These characteristics might all be good things in a last-resort, last-ditch effort to survive. But is it necessary to get into a fight with an armed intruder? What happens when an untrained person tries to engage an armed assailant using hand-to-hand combatives?

Normally, nothing pretty.

Is there something else that could be more effective?

There must be a "yes" to this question, especially when we're talking about schools and small children. But the concern also applies to any kind-hearted, untrained person. There has to be an alternative to fighting. And there is: distraction and dysfunction. The idea is that if we can find a way to disrupt how an opponent is thinking (like throwing a chair at their head), we give ourselves time to act... and escape.

The goal is the key. While the objective of "fight" is to disable your opponent, the goal of "defend" is to create options. Either disable your opponent or create an opportunity to act and escape.

What is so frustrating is that some schools, businesses, and government agencies are still practicing a static "lockdown" approach to violent intruder situations. All this practice re-enforces is our propensity to be an easy target. We can do better.

Move. Evade. Defend.

In May 2017, two people were fatally stabbed and a third was injured after a violent person on a commuter train began shouting slurs at two teenage girls. According to witnesses, the deceased individuals attempted to de-escalate the violent individual. When de-escalation failed, they stepped in front of the man, forming a barrier between the two girls and the aggressor. All three were slashed in the neck.

Any training for responding to violent events needs to address how escalation works. It needs to address how to respond to violence correctly, even if no one is being attacked yet. And all of us need to understand that any tool can be used as a deadly weapon. The outcome depends on whose hands are holding it. Never, ever assume that someone isn't capable and ready to seriously injure you.

Don't condition yourself so that you're only able to act correctly for an active shooter. Train for the violent intruder.

Emergency preparedness is typically broken down into two very broad categories: natural emergencies and manmade emergencies. We've been talking about manmade emergencies the most, but, without any doubt, *both* are increasing. 2017 was the most disastrous year on record in the United States, both in the number of natural disasters and the cost, which totaled more than 90 billion dollars more than any year prior. We had more disastrous fires, storms, and flooding than any other time in recorded history.

2017 was also the worst year on record for aggravated assaults in the US since 2009. According to the FBI, violent crime (rape, murder, assault, etc.) in 2016 (which is the most current year we have data for) increased within cities by about 10%. Every region within the nation (NW, NE, SW, SE) experienced an average increase of about 5% regarding violent events. It is an easy assumption that this upward trend continued through 2017.

Imagine this: you're walking along a busy road. It's spring. The day is clear and bright, the air is clean and fresh. Life is good. Peaceful. Can you see it?

Vroom. Vroom.

Every few seconds, a car zips by at 50 miles per hour.

You've walked along a busy road before. You've probably even done so with a complete level of calm despite the lethal objects zooming by every few seconds.

Every year, 30–40,000 pedestrians are stuck by cars and killed within the United States. Injury rates are even higher. Over 172,000 children (under the age of 14) were struck and injured by cars in 2013 alone.

Every time we walk along a roadway, there is the potential for injury and death. I know, it sounds like a terrible life perspective. But it's true.

My question is, how can we still enjoy life so much, even in such a dangerous situation?

If we can find the answer to this question, then perhaps we can apply the same principle to emergency preparedness, active killers, and violence. We can continue to enjoy life to this same degree even though these things are becoming more common in our world.

Here it is. This is key to emergency preparedness: to be successful, it is necessary to cultivate a culture that supports readiness and that is willing to invest in preparedness.

Almost all of us own at least one car. All of us go through required training and testing on how to drive and maintain a license. And, despite the fact that we all have cars sitting in driveways, we appreciate the dangers of them. We take steps to enact laws to keep us safe, install seatbelts and lights, and teach our children about the involved risks.

We have to treat emergency preparedness for both natural and manmade disasters the same way. We have to be willing to recognize that large-scale and individual traumatic events are happening and could happen to any one of us. But instead of being afraid of these things, we need to be ready. We need to educate our children about how to avoid these dangers, prevent them, and then act during them. We need to invest our time and resources into preparing ourselves and our loved ones, through quality training, mental conditioning, and physical preparedness.

As we ready ourselves for the unknown emergency event, we'll discover something remarkable: there is rest in the level of awareness and confidence that we have developed. Without a doubt, this level of preparedness takes time and it takes investment. But quality emergency preparedness absolutely reduces fear while empowering us to act with confidence during emergency situations.

On a final note, I see one additional tendency in violent intruder training classes worth discussing as we transition into the last and most important section of this book, *The Aftermath.*

Inevitably, in every mock scene that I conduct, participants pretend to be dead.

During advanced exercises, one of my instructors runs into the training building. He's wearing head-to-toe body armor. He's got a facemask on. A camo jacket. He's screaming threats. And he's got a fully automatic airsoft gun (it's empty).

It is amazing to see the effect that an empty airsoft gun has on people when they get "shot," even after just finishing eight hours of advanced training. They fall over. They writhe on the ground. They just... stop.

When I ask them why (and I always do), they give me the same answer, again and again: "I'm dead."

YOU ARE NOT DEAD!

In real-life gun battles, 86% of individuals struck in the abdominal cavity die from non-lethal wounds. To put it a different way and say it again: in the vast majority of traumatic violent incidences, individuals die from shock. <u>Shock</u>.

This is such a phenomenon that the National Trauma Institute has labeled shock as the second leading cause of death in traumatic injury cases.

That is unbelievable.

You are not dead. Get up. Move. Evade. Defend. Do something. Anything.

Believe that you can survive.

Let's talk about Rule Number One. It's not to go home at the end of each day.

Rule Number One is to be home *right now*. Whether you are looking down the barrel of a gun or walking alongside quiet waters, never stop believing in who the Master has made you to be. You are not dead.

Section Three: The Aftermath

Chapter Eight

Living in the Aftermath

Every time humans have developed a serious lethal weapon, we have simultaneously developed the ability to protect ourselves from the very threat we have created. With swords, we developed shields. Then thick leather armor. Then bronze armor. Then iron armor. Then full plate armor. With firearms, we went through a similar process, moving from soft-shell Kevlar armor to full-on ballistic plates and armored bomb suits.

Utilizing these protection tools requires preparation, however. Their effectiveness is dependent upon seeing the threat long in advance. The mental and physical preparation and training we have discussed so far is exactly the same. We prepare before the event so that we can either avoid the situation entirely or react effectively within it.

But, throughout history, the story consistently ends with the conclusion of the crisis moment. The hero just returns home and lives happily ever after.

As a culture— and perhaps even as a race—we have idolized the battle and forgotten about its lingering effects. Nobody wants to hear about what happens after the sparks are done flying and you go home. Part of the reason for this is that negative PR is bad for the propaganda business. The most eager recruits marching off to battle are the short-sighted ones.

The reason I bring this up is simple: if you have learned anything by reading this book, it is that you are in the middle of a battle. It's easy to forget during the mundane grind of life, but when the 3% day hits, it becomes all too clear. Most of you have already had a 3% kind of day in your life—if you've been robbed, assaulted, or had another violent event effect you. Statistically, the rest of you will have at least one 3% day before you leave this earth.

That is why we are going to be ready. We are going to be confident in who we are, what the vision of our life looks like, and who the Master is. We are going to be aware, trained, and ready to act when the time comes. We aren't going to be oblivious any longer.

We are going to live trained, live true, and live tactical.

But we also need to know how to come back home. When an active shooter strikes, all the workers eventually must go back to work. Students must go back to school. We must return to being fully alive.

For most, this last section of the violent story is the most difficult. It is also where there is the least support. After the mass casualty incident at Sandy Hook, the school demolished their entire building to try and help erase what happened. Seattle Pacific University spent over five million dollars renovating the building where the attack took place. This isn't about corporations or schools including recovery in their planned cost. It *is* all about people being able to continue on in life. Full life, to be precise.

If you've already had a violent or traumatic encounter in your life, you already know exactly what I'm talking about. If you are the rare person who hasn't, go down to your local VA. Meet the people who are still trying to come home after fifty long years. For most, the return home is never easy.

The foundation of this last, great hurdle is rooted in two things: identity and fear.

Most people who have experienced a violent encounter don't know who they really are. They haven't identified, clearly and concisely, the vision the Master has for their life. We started off this story seeking out the vision of the Master, for ourselves and for the world. I told you we needed to start there and I meant it.

You must ask and answer the hard questions about life before the 3% kind of day happens. The hard questions are these: What is worth dying for? What is worth living for?

The first is actually pretty simple to answer. You probably already know it.

I occasionally offer state licensing classes for firearms and other lethal-force weapon systems. Most states require some sort of certification class for police, security, and protection professionals for their lethal and less-than-lethal weapon systems. I tell all my trainees during class that the number one rule is to go home at the end of each day. It is my job to tell them this, and it is important I do so.

But I'm not going to tell *you* this.

For you and me, Rule Number One is not to go home at the end of each day. Rule Number One is to be fully alive, in every breath and heartbeat. We have a greater vision. When you are walking in line with the Master's vision, you are home. You are always going home. Even in death, if our vision is the true vision, we can believe that we are more than conquerors.

But the second question—what is worth living for?—is the more difficult question.

I'm challenging you in this section to ask that question. Ponder it. Seek out the truth of it. Think about it in the context of tomorrow being your 3% day.

Honestly, some of you will be terrified by what you find when you ask this question. You might realize that you are living amazingly average lives. You go to work, you come home. You clean the house, you go out with friends. You are tugged by addiction, enslaved by lust, chained by things you can't seem to control.

If this is you when (not *if*) the 3% day happens, your world will be turned upside down.

During my training classes, when talking about seeking out the vision of the Master for our lives, I call it "spiritual fitness." Spiritual fitness is a decision you make every day because it is about being fully alive in light of the Master's objective truth.

When you encounter a lethal-force confrontation, one of three things will typically happen: you die, you barely escape while others don't, or you kill your enemy. Whichever way it goes, you are left with the outcome and you need to be ready for it. If you kill your enemy, you need to recognize that you just immersed yourself in one of the most deeply traumatic experience that exists for mankind. If you survive, you need to be able to come to terms with it and live with it. If you die... well, you're dead.

I'll tell you, if you are not fully alive now, you will be in serious trouble in every one of those circumstances.

In any emergency, the planning phase is not the difficult part. Being able to mentally comprehend the truth of your circumstances and shift into action is always the challenge.

So, what is the truth of our circumstances? What is worth living for and where do I find it? Truly, these questions are the key to recovery, just as they are the key to all of emergency preparedness. Remember, when our strength has failed, we are defined by whatever we have made master over our lives. Being able to articulate exactly what this means will be the foundation for any hope of recovery we have. We need a master who can be a firm foundation, even in the face of death.

Let us come back to the obvious question that has remained unanswered throughout this book: who is your master? Is there only one True Master? Can objective truth be boiled down to a single focal point that remains true across cultures and time, or is it just floating out there somewhere amidst the trees?

Identifying the True Master is, without any doubt, the foundation of preparedness and the key to real, healthy recovery after a traumatic event.

I think the best way to identify the Master is by looking at fractals embedded in our earliest recorded histories, histories which document the beginning of our supernatural vision.

A fractal is a mathematical term, defined as an infinitely recurring pattern that is unexplainable: "unpredictable in specific details yet deterministic when viewed as a total pattern." A common example would be the recurring, perfect pattern of a snowflake produced in a winter storm, or the electrical current produced by a lightning bolt, or the swirling nature of a galaxy. The closer you look at these objects the more you see the same thing, simply repeated in smaller variations through a perfect design.

When we are seeking objectivity, we must start by looking at deterministic events when viewed as a whole. Are there recurring patterns of objective truth that show up throughout history?

Chapter Nine

A Whisper Through Time

Just like a fractal, the fundamental stories of our most ancient history have strikingly similar patterns. Investigating the roots of those ancient stories may lead us to the Master and a context for recovery that even our earliest ancestors understood.

Many of our most ancient civilizations developed separately, divided by mountains and oceans. They had no contact and no sharing of legends or tales regarding who the Master is, how creation and the world began, or what man's objective within the story of life could be.

The oldest histories known to man are attributed to our earliest civilizations, circa 10,000-3,000 BCE, and are recorded in ancient documents of proto and cuneiform writing. Of course, if we believe in the macro-evolution of different humanoids, wouldn't all of these isolated groups of people have very different beliefs and histories as they separately rationalized their creation?

They would.

Unless they all came from the same place. From the same master. And had the same vision written upon the tablets of their hearts.

Let's take a look at the fractals of history as they were

recorded from across vast geographic divides.

Sumerian Civilization (Mesopotamian Valley):

Historians agree that the fertile crescent was the birthplace of civilization. As the history of the city of Jericho attests, the cities in this area had walls, culture, and written language as early as the Neolithic Era (10,000-7000 BCE). We'll never know how these peoples thought or walked upon the earth, but we know they fished from boats, domesticated large animals, hunted with bows and spears, and worked wood and stone into intricate forms with chisels and gouges. They smelt and cast precious metals into complex designs, used number systems, charted the stars into 12 lunar months, and developed the first systems of agriculture.

We also know that whatever sort of man existed before this era, this transition into culture happened rapidly. Cities were built suddenly and rapidly where none had previously existed. Such rapid advancement has only similarly been seen in the Industrial Revolution, which attests to the level of intelligence and competence these ancient peoples possessed. Fortunately, through the Sumerians' early development of proto and cuneiform writing, much of what these most ancient peoples believed about themselves and the world is still known.

The first and most consistent fractal among all ancient peoples is a reverence for the Master. This can be seen in the fact that the first White Temple was built in the city of Uruk during this period. It stood on a terrace forty feet high, and estimates suggest that it took more than 1500 workers over 5 years to complete the structure.

Clearly, both rulers and peoples were willing to invest their time, resources, and will into the pursuit of walking with the Master. Doesn't that seem strange, when all those people and hours could have been better spent securing food, waging wars, or plowing fields?

In fact, historians agree that the single, most deeply

engrained mark of these people was their religious qualities. Without any doubt, the people of early Mesopotamia shared an honored vision of the Master.

The ancient Sumerians believed that all they knew had been revealed to them by the gods, which were like in form to man. A single infinite being called Anu, Lord of the Sky, created all other deities and forms from a void of shapeless nothing (*abzu*). Anu had two sons, or forms, called Enlil and Enki, who were worshiped as the Lord of Earth and the Lord of Waters. Together, Anu, Enlil, and Enki made a triune godhead that was of the same blood.

From these three beings came other lesser gods, from whom creation began through a divine consensus. Yet the decision was not unanimous: another being, Tiamat, the dragon of chaos, along with a cohort of other lesser divine beings, waged battle in the unseen heavens (*chaoskampf*).

Man was highly impacted by this battle. Droughts, infertility, and human battles were all echoes of other-worldly, greater battles raging. Stele's of the ancient Sumerians depict the wars of kings over-shadowed by raging battles of heavenly forces.

An inherent element in all these stories is that mankind had somehow upset the order laid down by the gods, and that man was ever striving to regain the original vision. Rites, sacrifices, and honored celebrations were some of the ways man tried to breach the divide between themselves and the gods.

The most ancient tales of the Sumerians include Utnapishtim, the only survivor of a multi-year flood which destroyed the entire world, and a snake that snatches away the long-lived, eternal years of man from Gilgamesh. This summary does not do these peoples justice, but it hints at the echoes that are preserved regarding what these people experienced and believed.

Native American (Mesoamerican) Civilization:
Thousands of miles away from the fertile crescent, separated

by countless mountain ranges and vast oceans, grew the cultures of the ancient Mayans and Aztecs. Both of these peoples came from an earlier Mesoamerican culture known as the Olmec, who were builders of great cities circa 1,500-400 BCE. These early peoples were also intelligent innovators, independently working precious metals, creating cities, playing vast gaming sports, and developing agriculture suitable for their jungle environment.

Yet there were many differences between them and their Mesopotamian counterparts. Mesoamericans did not domesticate large animals, for example, and they did not utilize the wheel.

The earliest documents of the Mesoamericans were discovered by Catholic missionaries in the 1500s, upon first contact with the New World by Spain . They were considered falsehoods and were destroyed. But a few hidden codices survived: the Popol Vuh, the Grolier, and the Dresden codex are a few. Perhaps they can shed light on the fractal we are seeking.

Historians agree that the Olmec, and thereafter the Mayans and the Aztecs, were fundamentally a religious people. Their sacrifices and their 365-day calendar of four ages dominated every aspect of the cultures.

The most ancient Mesoamericans believed that thirteen layers of heaven rose above the earth, with nine levels of the underworld stretching below. The Ometeotl, the supreme creator of all, dwelt in the heavens. This god was a god of duality, simultaneously one god in several forms, both male and female; As the earth complements the sky, the Mesoamericans believed this god complemented himself.

Before creation, chaos reigned like a mist shifting above waters. Yet within the mist there was Ometeotl, and Ometeotl began to speak. As he spoke, the things he said came into being. First from Ometeotl came four other gods, who separated the earth and the heavens and stood like mighty trees at the four corners of the world. Then came the vision of how life should be—how the trees and animals would exist, and how mankind would be the centerpiece of them all.

Another account of the Mixtec people (who lived alongside and sometimes paid tribute to the Aztec) says that this dualistic god created a garden of magical trees and flowers that mankind walked in. Another account describes the first forms of man as immortals who had the ability to see the future as clearly as the gods, until the gods breathed upon them and literally fogged their vision like a mirror.

Within all of these accounts rise other, lesser gods, who were both individualistic and part of group—either a group of protagonist gods, or a group of antagonist gods. And, as you may have guessed, mankind was intimately involved in their battle. The center of this entire region was built around temples, rites, and sacrifices as the people strove to regain congruence within the heavenly system.

One repeated story throughout Mesoamerican culture tells of how all the waters of the sky and the waters of the underworld came and filled the entire earth for 52 years, until even the tops of mountains disappeared. Then a new age of mankind began.

Amazing.

Seeing any fractals yet?

Indian (Indus Valley) & Chinese (Yellow River) Civilizations:

The ancient histories of India and prehistoric China are two that I will lump together because not as much evidence remains of these earliest cultures. The written word of the early Indian civilization remains unreadable, and while some compelling evidence can be taken from later oral traditions that likely passed down from this era, we should be careful to preserve the integrity of our research.

Most historians agree that Mesopotamian culture had some impact on the early cultures of the Indus valley. There is clear evidence of trade between the two from an early time.

The earliest god discovered in the Indus Valley was a three-headed god, flanked by animals and sitting in a yoga position that has similar qualities to the later god, Shiva. According to later tradition, Shiva was one of three creator gods: Brahma, Shiva, and Vishnu. Brahma was considered the Lord of Speech, Shiva the Lord of Energy and Power, and Vishnu a spirit of Brahma. These three-in-one gods brought the universe into being from the darkness of nothing (*tamas*), while Vritra (the dragon and adversary) attempted to overthrow the heavenly hosts.

Early China proves to be more fruitful than the Indus Valley at this earliest stage of civilization, merely because more evidence that can be understood survives in that region. Historians agree that the first men living on the Yellow River in China had no outside influences whatsoever. Our main source of writing has been discovered upon oracle bones and is attributed to the first four dynasties of Chinese civilization: The Xia, Shang, Hsia, and Chou dynasties, circa 2,500 BCE. Each oracle bone would carry a few thousand characters of the first known ancient Chinese script, giving the earliest insight into this civilization's customs and beliefs. It is worth noting that, within all early cultures, our most consistent artifacts remain of religious significance. These early peoples unanimously felt that they needed to rely upon a greater vision.

Of most prominence on these bones is the god Shang Ti, "Ruler Above." The peoples of the Yellow River believed that Shang Ti was the absolute god of the universe, ruler over all other spiritual beings. They believed he was intimately involved in things affecting man, such as battles, harvests, and nature. Shang Ti was considered so holy that sacrifices could not be directly offered to him—they had to be offered to dead ancestors who would then intercede on the behalf of the living.

During this time, another story was recorded: the Great Flood of Gun-Yu. This event allegedly lasted for two generations during the Xia dynasty, which was later succeeded by the Shang dynasty. Again in China, we see temples, sacrifices, and daily rites showing us that these earliest peoples' daily lives were dedicated to re-establishing harmony with the heavenly hosts.

Seeing any fractals now?

Image 7. Map of Isolated Ancient Civilizations

There are still other regions of the world worth noting, such as isolated regions of Africa and Australia, which you should look up on your own. Due to the lack of writing in these regions, oral tradition is prevalent. Keeping in mind how colonial influences can change oral traditions over time, I have left these out of our conversation in an attempt to find a truly pure, ancient fractal.

Even with such a brief look at these ancient stories, I see a few key patterns:

1.   Every ancient group of people on the face of the planet was deeply ingrained with a belief that they were created by a single being who has a relationship with himself

in an acceptably contradictory way (multiple personalities in one), who is both present and remote, and who is lord over all.

2.   Every ancient history of these beings describes one who represents darkness, who hates the good and the light, and who wishes to destroy them.

3.   Every group of people recognized a separation between their gods and man, and this separation affects everyday needs such as food, nature, and living. They also tried to appease the gods, typically by requiring some type of blood sacrifice.

4.   Very specific, supernatural stories exist cross-culturally, such as that of a flood that destroys the world.

The more ancient histories you look at, the more fractals you'll see. The deeper into these documents and cultures you dive, the more you'll be shocked at how similar the stories get the farther back you go.

How is this possible? Is it reasonable to think that groups of isolated peoples were able to create and then intimately believe the exact same stories about their most ancient history, origins, and involvement in a supernatural battle?

Doesn't it seem strange that not a single ancient group of people within these cultures lacks a supernatural vision from a master creator? Doesn't it seem odd that all these stories are, at their core, the same stories? Seriously, what are the mathematical, objective odds that fractals like these could occur by chance?

The odds are impossible.

In fact, the odds are so impossible that it seems like the only thing mankind has been able to agree on for the last 10,000 years or so is that we are deeply entwined in a supernatural, spiritual battle.

Can a rational human argue with quantum physics, with the fractals of history, and with the revelation vision that has touched lives across the world? Can we honestly say there is no objective, supernatural master?

We can't. There must be a master, and the question that brought us to this point remains the same: in the darkness of recovery after the violent event, what will give you strength? What will be your firm foundation?

The best argument I've heard from an atheist attempting to explain the process of creation and the existence of objective truth was through this contradictory statement: "Well, creation wasn't *all* random. There was a guiding force that made the process more likely. We call it natural selection."

You can't naturally select *anything* if nothing is there. That is avoiding the question. We are not discussing evolution or change over time. We are talking about the beginning of an objective, supernatural vision. The one we can't seem to get away from.

The problem with all arguments against a maker's presence in the vision of our lives is the same: they are founded on the idea that objective truth came into being through a random process. That nothing existed, and then something enduringly true began and continues to exist through random selection.

Despite the obvious conflict of mathematical odds, history, and common sense, this non-committal ideology dominates in western culture. Even individuals who believe in a greater vision and in one True Master often fall into the Venus flytrap of not really committing either way. Why bother answering the tough questions about who the Master is? Why commit one way or the other? Does it matter, really?

These questions lead down an easier road, but it's a perilous blindfold that falls to tatters during the critical violent event.

Where do these questions leave us during recovery? Where do they leave us when we're faced with death? I'll tell you truly, they leave us nowhere. They leave us living in condition white; the end result is a short trip into the oblivion of Code Black.

Our culture works so hard to get away from an objective

vision because having one means that people aren't in control of their own lives. In our modern world, it seems like we all have to be able to choose everything for ourselves and create our own destiny. No wonder our younger generations seem to be having difficulty standing upon moral, objective principles. The world is telling them there aren't any.

Even now, with all our technology and knowledge, is our modernized educational view of creation any different than a supernatural story? A flash of energy, light, heat, and then... boom. It's all there in a few microseconds. Because, of course, what existed before creation wasn't based on the principles of time. Funny. That sounds like eternity. That sounds very god-like. That sounds like a fractal of the same story I'm seeing recorded in 6,000 BCE. But dare we make that stark connection in our classrooms? No—we wouldn't want to offend anyone with the idea of objective truth.

It is a deep flaw in our current educational system.

No sane person argues against objective truth. Only those who are afraid of what it might mean to have a master over the vision of their lives. There's just no way around it. Just like the violent traumatic event, we can't outrun it. We can't outfight it. We must turn and face it.

Chapter Ten

The Name of the Master

We are trying to pinpoint the objectively true vision for our lives. We know that doing so will make recovery easier, swifter, and more effective. And we've decided that the best way to get there is by identifying the Master. In our modern-day culture, it is hard to see a deterministic pattern through the unpredictable details. Yet, when we look back through the specifics—even in our earliest recorded histories—we see common whispers.

The world is full of patterns and clues that point to the Master—objective truths inlayed within the bedrock of creation. Ironically, the word "fractal" stems from the Latin word *fractus*, which means "broken." Perhaps there is even an internal pattern hinting at a greater reality.

Before we can recover, and, I would dare to say, before we can be truly prepared for the emergency event, we MUST have a firm handle on who this Master is. We MUST have an objective reality to guide our hearts and minds in combat. If you don't have this vision, why waste your time fighting to protect others? For the "greater good of mankind"? Because it's the "right thing to do"? You see, it will always come back to this objective vision we have ingrained on our hearts. The Master's vision for your life is calling you to wake up and become fully alive.

I've always been shocked by how powerful names are. My name means "one who is constantly vigilant," and it is such an accurate picture of my character. I have spent long hours thinking about the names of my children so that they might live into the power of them.

In ancient times, when people had a stark revelation regarding the vision for their life, they would often receive a new name. This new name could come from a king, giving it to a prisoner in light of their new identity, for example, or it could come from God.

The word "name" is defined as "a set of words by which something is known." We know there is a Master. But we need to know who this master is. We need to start looking for the Master's name. Maybe then we'll be able to find our own name and better identify the vision of our lives.

Ancient history points us to the Master and gives us some fundamental basics on what the Master must look like. I see fractals of a triune godhead; a key spiritual enemy; and a separation, a brokenness between peoples and their god that they have consistently tried—and consistently failed—to bridge through good works and sacrifice. But this ancient history doesn't give us a modern look at who the Master *really* is. What is this Master's name today, tomorrow, and in my life this very moment when I need to see the vision?

Various religions claim to have an inside ear on the Master's name and attribute various characteristics to who they believe the Master is. Problem is, when I look at the vast majority of religions, I see a very, very big gap between the practices that these religions require and the name of the Master I'm looking for.

Yet, religious institutions are key parts of modern, healthy crisis-response support. Spiritual fitness is the foundation of recovery and the start of healing. It is best practice.

So, which religions have the inner ear on the truth? And what do I have to do after I find the truth? This is where things get interesting and most people get bogged down. I'm not surprised—most of the time, I feel bogged down by manufactured ideas of religion as well. But we are set free by the vision of the King. It is worth sifting through to find. Remember, we have a tendency as humans to simply throw in the towel and settle for less when things get hard. We cannot do that here. We must stay the course if we are going to be prepared for the violent encounter.

When sifting through modern religion, you only need to ask one, two-part question to see the name of its master clearly:

What is being offered and what is required?

Various religions offer all sorts of things. I don't need or want magical powers, strange hallucinations, or voices. Truth be told, I have no desire to live forever. I'm not looking to buy anything, and I know I can't earn my way into a holy vision. To be bluntly honest, I just want to be alive. Fully alive, right now in every breath and from now on, even after the worst day of my life. I know that this is what comes from walking with the True Master.

I want to make sure I'm fighting the right battle and wielding my sword as I should. I want to see the Master's vision for my life so I can follow it. I want the truth, the same truth that reigned over my ancient ancestors and that will reign over my children. Capital T-Truth, and I'll take it and follow it in any form it comes in. I want to know the Master's name so I can be one with his vision. All else is secondary. All else is downright unimportant.

That cuts down the list of religious propagandas dramatically.

There are a few belief systems out there that claim the Master is no longer involved in our lives. The Master started creation and then left us to our own demise. Just by gauging the status of this broken world, I can see why some would think that, and it's an idea worth addressing.

But all it takes is one true miracle, one breathtaking, supernatural event in the entirety of history to prove this thesis false. Just by looking at my own life, I can attest that this principle is invalid. When I include others... well, let's just say it's very, very clear that both the Master and an enemy are still at work in astonishing ways in the world.

Other religions out there seem to have the same, fundamental problem. They require their servants to complete a long, tedious series of actions to become in line with the vision of the Master. These religions provide a checklist of key elements their subjects must complete to attain "spiritual enlightenment" or something similar.

Imagine this: write down a description of a gun. Then stick that description onto a piece of steel and wait for it to change. Go ahead and write out all the necessary steps for it to become a gun. Be detailed. It needs to heat itself, beat itself into shape, sand itself, put on a nice polish, temper itself, quench itself, assemble itself... okay, you get the point. How long will it take until that piece of steel reaches your vision? See the problem?

It's not going to happen unless the maker actually gets involved.

It is completely ridiculous to say that you or I can directly bring about a supernatural vision for our lives on our own. We know there is a maker. I need to find him to find the vision. But I can't make that vision happen in my life without the Maker's involvement.

I am looking for a religion that points me towards a historical, supernatural, yet realistic world—one where the Master is intimately involved in my life, actually working on molding me into his vision.

In addition, it is only logical that coming face to face with the Master of Objective Truth would re-define our subjective principles and give new light to more powerful, objective ones.

Like describing color to a blind man and then having that man suddenly see, there is a dramatic difference between objective reality and the whispers of it. Shocking, earth-shattering differences.

When I look for the Master and the vision he has for my life, I look for these earth-shattering objective truths. Truths that plant my feet on firm soil, set my mortal mind reeling, and at the same time cause my spirit to soar to new heights. Remember, I'm looking for life. Full life. Right now. In my body, mind, and heart, for they are all connected. As you experience the truth, it will affect your entire being, often in a way you did not expect.

There is only one religion, one group of people claiming to know the Master's name, that makes sense regarding all the elements of truth we are seeking. My search for the Master began in the jungles of Guatemala, led me down the roads of ancient history, and dumped me in a little town called Nazareth in the year that Jesus Christ was born.

I'll tell you why.

The beliefs of ancient Hebrews are rooted in the most ancient religion of mankind: the religion practiced by the Sumerians. Therefore, Christianity is in tune with the fractals of history, expressing a triune Godhead, historical supernatural events, and an enemy who seeks to destroy the good in the world.

Yet, there is one element unique to Christianity that is not duplicated in any other place.

A key facet of every fractal we have seen is the assumption of a separation, a divide between the gods and man. Throughout the ages, mankind has been struggling to close the wound and restore the divide, thus regaining the vision of their maker. But how can man bridge a divine gap?

This divide echoes in every history mankind possesses, and it is where all religions wane. Somehow, mankind was intimately involved in the spiritual and we were uncannily separated. How that separation occurred is not a question for this book, yet some piece within all of us still longs for that vision.

We catch glimpses here and there in the physical world where that whispered vision of a supernatural dance leaps out at us, stirring our hearts with wonder and glory. But ever does it slip away, and the stark reality of the physical world takes its place. Like a dream fading in our minds, we seem to remember ...and long for... the ancient power of the Master.

The ancient Hebrews understood the supernatural vision and recognized this separation. They, like many other religions of the ancient world, offered blood sacrifices, believing that only the spirit of life had the power to help heal this holy wound.

But it was never enough. And they knew it.

If you are looking for the vision of the Master, you go to the Master. If you are looking to *be* the vision of the Master, nothing on this earth will take you there. He has to come to you. That is the fundamental fractal of history and what we need to look for when seeking out the name of our Master.

Through prophecy, the Hebrews clung to a promise: that one day, the Master himself would come and bridge this divide. He would make all things right. He would once again bring full life.

Literally.

They knew the Master had to come to them if they were going to be delivered unto the point of physically, emotionally, and spiritually finding full life again. That the Master would bridge this gap is a mind-boggling concept, but it aligns with the fractals of history and the most powerful fractals of nature, which are themselves clear echoes of the Master's design.

Prophecies that the Master would come in the flesh of man are recorded throughout ancient history. By the hand of David, circa 1,000 BCE; by Isaiah, 800 years before the time of Christ; by Daniel, 600 years before Jesus walked the earth; by Ezekiel, 580 years before the Lord entered the physical world; and by many, many others.

These baffling, archaeologically verified prophecies show physical man enough in tune with the spiritual realm to predict the very day Jesus would enter Jerusalem for his death and to precisely pinpoint the location he would be pierced long before crucifixion had ever been used. They are proof enough of the supernatural, all by themselves.

How, though, could the Master enter into the physical world? What would it be like? How would it change things? What would the culmination of objective truth look like in the physical realm?

By definition, the Hebrews knew it would change everything.

It is not above man's conception to promote himself to the status of a god. That has happened throughout history and always for the same purpose: power. Specifically, power over the lives of others. Of course, who has more power than the Master? There is none. And this is exactly what the Jews thought the Messiah would look like: a king, robed in power, delivering them from the overlord of death by destroying their enemies and bringing them finally into the Master's vision as conquering heroes.

Hey, that sounds pretty good.

But remember, like the blind seeing color for the first time, the first sight of the Master should defy any mortal conception. He should, in one deft sweep, accomplish more than any thought possible in a way we never could have imagined. He should fulfill one reality while creating an entirely new one. Logically speaking, he should renew the possible through the impossible. Make the smallest things the largest, the poorest the richest.

Plausibly, an objective god turned physical would turn the world on its head if it did not align with his vision. Just like a piece of steel in a hot forge, the properties of the unseen would pass into the seen with a result that no one could fathom.

During the time of Jesus, the law was "an eye for an eye... a hand for a hand." Kingdoms rose and fell, driven by the blood of kings and the bodies of slaves. Of course, the Jews thought the Master would arrive as a king, with status, wealth, and power. How else would he lead his people and overthrow their enemies?

But that was the problem. Their vision was much too small. The Jews were steel in the fire. What they failed to see was that their enemies were as well. The Master had a vision for them all—for all of creation. For you and me.

The culmination of the world's fractals is a god who brings life back to his people. Not by the works of our hands: but by the piercing of his own.

Jesus says, "I have come so that you may have full life, and life to its fullest."

That is exactly what we have been looking for.

On the 3% day, when the Mossberg Shotgun is leveled at your head, there is no certainty that you will survive. You must be able to find yourself, even in that most horrible of places, at peace. This is the vision of the Master: it is the redemption of our brokenness through Jesus, even in the face of death.

That is why knowing the name of the Master is so critical when facing the violent traumatic encounter. He came. He bled. He died. He chose this path, remaining Lord over all. He set you free so that even within your worst moments, you might live.

As a blacksmith, if I wanted to empower a lump of high-carbon steel to believe that it had the capacity to be a sword in my hand, there would be only one way I could communicate my vision to it: I would have to become it. I would have to voluntarily suffer the fire, then emerge as a new creation. Only then would my lump of steel recognize and believe its true potential, even under the scorching heat of the fire.

Visions are not described by fact, for the facts of the vision transcend our comprehension. They are described by allegory and by example, for they must free our minds to obtain more than we could ever dream.

Jesus condemned himself to our weakest moments in the name of freeing us to live out a greater vision, even within the suffering of our lives today. He came to us and told us who he was. He showed us through signs and wonders. He told us the future. He pushed our minds to grasp his vision, using allegory and story. Yet it had to be more than that. He had to walk alongside us in a new way, a way that was not possible before. He needed to melt our old vision and re-cast us into a new image.

Before Jesus, the law of the land was equal vengeance through power.

Jesus showed us that the name of the Master is transcendent justice through redemption and love.

There are few things that affect all of us equally. Death is one of them. Jesus showed us that the Master's vision, his vision, was greater. It is a supernatural vision that is more commanding than the culminating power of the physical realm.

It is a vision, a life, that endures over death.

An upheaval of exponential magnitude would have to accompany a moment in which the Master physically walks upon the earth. And like one might expect from such a stark, objective truth covertly inserting itself into this broken world, the life, death, and renewal of Christ produced a shock-wave that cannot be described in any other fashion.

Those that walked with him utterly changed. They believed in something that held undeniable power. Through torture, death, and humiliation, those people that believed in him remained entirely new creations—new people in the same body, as though the physical world retained little influence over them.

In fact, the world grew afraid of the stark, blooming power they suddenly saw crashing over the land like water from a breaking dam. The leaders in control tried to stop it. Some are still trying. Literally overnight, cities turned from death and believed in the vision of the Master. They believed his name, and they found the vision we have all been missing.

The life and death of Jesus of Nazareth has been the single most world-changing moment in recorded history. There is no comparison. Really. There is a reason why the clock starts at 1 AD. It was the beginning of a new age. An age of the Master's revealed vision.

I call seeing this vision and walking this path the "high road." It's a tough road to find and an even tougher one to walk. Most people look at their feet when they are on a tough road. You are on a tough road, but you are no longer blind. All have had the truth of who the Master is written upon their hearts. You know it. You have felt it. And if you believe in it, your road toward recovery will have a place where the burdens of this world will lose their power.

Chapter Eleven

Shield Wall

The Master has placed a vision of what is right, good, and true upon our heart. It's not just what is fair, it is what is supernaturally good. But we all have a choice. You have a special gift, and the gift I'm talking about isn't life. It is the freedom to choose between the light and the dark.

Each history has a light and a dark and a powerful being that (while created for good) chose the darkness. Like a fractal, ancient Greek, Sumerian, Egyptian, Hebrew, Hindu, and Native American civilizations all share a different version of the same story. And now we face the same choice. Is this all legend and myth? Or is this a truth that has affected the world and our hearts so deeply that we all remember it to our core?

This truth has not only affected our personal lives, but the world as a whole. You recognize the need to be strong of heart, of mind, and of body. You've seen the vision the Master has for your life.

Be careful, here. Too many people have gotten this far and decided to go out on their own... and the enemy snuck up and buried them. The danger of pursuing the vision of what the Master has placed upon your heart without guidelines has been seen time and time again. You have all heard the stories: the men and women who claim to hear the voice of the Master telling them to do something that is, quite simply, evil. Or untrue. Even more common is the "spiritual visionary," who takes a bit of objective truth and mixes it in with all sorts of subjective opinions.

This is one of the enemy's oldest tricks, and he is very effective at it. There is good reason why the enemy was known in the Ancient Days as the "deceiver." It is much easier to create a false master than it is to get rid of the real one.

To train successfully, you need a sensei. A teacher. You need to remember your original vision so you don't get lost in the woods of the enemy's attacks. We are going to talk about two of my favorite ways to remember the vision the Master has given us: studying the Word and being sharpened by others on the high road.

The written word has always held great power. Our most ancient stories tell us (almost unanimously) that the Master spoke creation into being. I don't think that is a typo or an allegorical statement. I think it is as true as statements get.

There are some that would argue that the most definitive, distinct characteristic of humankind is the ability to communicate through language. Language is conveyed through nonverbal, verbal, and written mediums. All three are important to understand when talking about combative training.

When the fires of life flare up, it is tough to remember your original vision. Every good blacksmith has pieces of soapstone and chalk scattered over his shop floor, because even when soapstone gets hot it is still visible on the steel the blacksmith is working. The vision can be drawn out and won't disappear in the fire.

We use written words and markings to remember the vision for all sorts of things. When you are lost, you read a map. You find the instruction manual. Or you wander around lost until you are humbled.

The vision of your identity is rooted in the name of the Master and in the story of his work in the world. Every historical record captures bits and pieces of this masterpiece. Every piece of work, piece of art, or piece of history can inspire you to remember the vision and calling for your life.

But there is only one compilation of work that paints a picture of history and allegory that the Master has used for thousands of years to reach billions of people. Don't write that off, pun intended. Remember, the Master wants to establish his vision with you and the world. When we find something that has great power and that has shaped and molded the world, we should look at it more closely.

In the case of the Bible, there is no question that it is the most powerful written document among all of mankind since the history of man began. Accredited sources tell us that over 6.7 billion copies of the Bible are in circulation today. The next two runners up both have about 900 million copies in circulation: the *Qur'an* and Chairman Mao's *Quotations*.

Chairman Mao's *Quotations*, often called the "little red book," is an inspirational political book published by the Communist Party of China in the 1960s. It was originally intended as daily readings for the People's Liberation Army. Interesting. I'm not sure this book counts, since for decades this document was a requirement for every Chinese citizen to read, own, and study. Unless you wanted to be imprisoned. Who wants to move to China?

For a moment let's all be grateful for the freedom of speech. We're talking about how powerful words are: what happens when that power is abused, controlled, and manipulated? The result can be catastrophic. Just thinking about it makes me want to start training: some things are worth fighting to protect.

The *Qur'an* was written after 600 AD and reflects Muhammad's interpretation of the Bible. There is no other way to put it. It is open knowledge that the Qur'an is about

Muhammad's vision (he even calls himself the messenger), similarly to how the Book of Mormon is a reflection of Joseph Smith's vision. Naturally, the reflection is not as strong as the source, and the source of both these texts (regardless of the accuracy of their reflection) is the Bible. Muhammad starts off his vision by tying in, as best as he can, to the vision of Noah, Abraham, and Jesus. Muhammad himself at least saw a glimpse of the truth, for he quotes Jesus: "Fear Allah and obey me (Jesus)."

Jesus wasn't a messenger. He wasn't a prophet. From the most ancient, historical texts we possess, Jesus used the same words that the Master used to introduce himself to Moses from the burning bush:

"I tell you the solemn truth, before Abraham came to be, I am."

Jesus was the Authority, the Redeemer, the ultimate fractal of history, and the Living God. This is not man's claim about Jesus. It is Jesus's claim about himself.

The Bible is the only textual source that does not claim to be the vision of a man, but the vision of the Master.

Could it be so? Could the fractals of the world, the whisper of history, and the call upon our hearts to live into his unique vision all culminate in this, the Master's name?

Find the True Master and make him king over your life.

My point in bringing up these two texts is to compare their power and influence in light of the power and influence of the Bible scriptures. It seems remarkably clear that the Bible is the most impactful text that has ever existed. It is the oldest. It is the foundation. It is the light in a dark place.

Interpretations and applications of what is listed in the Bible varies as much as people do. Listed within is the most accurate picture of the Master's objective truth, the fractals of history, and the prophecies of the Master's guidance. It gets the closest to physically describing something that is, by nature, impossible to physically describe.

More importantly, it is a story of the Master's vision for you. From direct principles to analogies that point us toward objective morals, we find the Bible to be the guiding light of the vision for us and for our neighbor.

But it is also more than that. It is essential to our vision and to the problem of mankind that the Master is intimately involved in our story. He needs to be able to directly shape us into his image. He needs to be able to work us within the fire of life.

Every good student, be it within martial arts or music, has a good teacher. And that teacher conveys his vision to the student through the power of communication. What would it look like if the Master himself could communicate to us directly through the written word? What if he could show us his name directly? By default, it would be something challenging.

It would have to be allegory and factual, both at once. It would transcend our comprehension while being perfectly in tune with history. It would be an eternal foundation that our forgetful, distracted minds could come back to for rest, revitalization, and sometimes a kick in the head to get us back in line with the vision.

The Master cares for his creation just like you care about what *you* invest in. His Bible shows us the way and helps us stay on it.

The Master has gone on record regarding his vision for our lives.

One of my favorite parts of the Bible is when the Master shares his name for the first time. I have a tough time reading it. I get flashes of PTSD from when I first learned the Master's name. It's in a section of the Bible called Exodus, when a man named Moses is called by the Master to lead his people. Moses has a speech impediment; He doesn't think he's up for the task. To convince him otherwise, the Master shares his vision—his name, actually—with Moses.

To those of you that still believe this whole Bible-vision thing is hocus-pocus and who use the counter-evidence of "historical" dates to contradict the story of Exodus, you need to do some real research on Egyptology. A good place to start is David Rohl's works (1995, 2007), as well as the new kingdom Canaanite presence in Egypt. Amazingly, history adds up with the Bible (a historical text). Yet, once again, our culture just likes letting people choose for themselves... and they shy away from connecting a holy vision to history like it is the plague—which is why this isn't taught in our K-12 schools. You have to get to a university or do some hard independent research before you find it. Shocking.

Studying the Bible is critical for us to do on a regular basis, especially when we start getting off our sofa and going out into the battle of the world. The world is full of subjective opinions. It is the stronghold of the enemy who wants to destroy you, who wants to blind you with lust, laziness, and lies. We need to seek out the truth of ourselves, the Master, and the world, and there is no better place to set your foundation than the Bible.

All combative training starts by seeking the truth. We have been seeking the truth together, about ourselves and the world, for quite a while. Once we find it, we have to grow in it. Nothing changes overnight. Human beings are creatures of repetition and of habit. We have to intentionally change, learning and growing through discipline and faithfulness.

I am never going to be in line with the Master's vision if I am only checking off the boxes of my spirituality. Rather, shouldn't I expect to pursue the Master's vision with discipline, faithfulness, and sacrifice? It makes sense that the vision of the Master will prompt me—even require me—to change, to become one with the vision (after all, the heart, body, and mind are all intimately connected).

But will I ever have that bridge fully crossed by the strength of my own hands?

Just like in good combatives, the further you progress, the

131

more you realize how much is left to learn. In theology, this is called sanctification: a life-long process of being molded into the Master's vision.

Learning how to execute a triangle choke from a defensive position is a task that takes a lot of time and energy—unless you have someone who's done it before, showing you the moves.

Human beings are all audio, visual, kinesthetic learners. Basically, that means we learn best from someone else: listening to them, watching them, and having them physically walk alongside us as we learn and grow. This journey always starts with us seeking the truth and laying down our burdens at the Master's feet. It must, absolutely must, involve others coming alongside us to help us in the journey.

Every once in a while, I meet followers of Jesus that don't believe in community. They are "do it themself-ers," and I respect that. In fact, I'm one of them: I would much rather go out and fight the battle on my own. But, when I'm honest, it's only because of two reasons. The first is that I don't like sharing my emotions with others. That second is that humans are messy, which makes it very easy to stray from the Master's vision.

Trust, love, accountability... these things are all great, and they are all really hard to do well. They take a lot of energy. They take a lot of investment in other people.

There is an old wives' tale that is told in martial arts. It tells of a not-so-great martial artist. He trained by himself every day. All day. He developed his own techniques, his own style of fighting. He walked the hard road and he stuck to it with discipline and commitment. But he didn't bring anyone alongside him, to refine him or mold him. One day, he thought he was ready. He walked into a dojo, a place where students and masters come together, and challenged anyone to attempt to defeat him.

He was defeated by the most basic of students. The masters didn't even waste their time.

Know why? Because it's easy to go out on your own. It doesn't require any commitment. You can only push yourself as far as you are willing.

It is *not* easy to humble yourself to the point of allowing someone else to teach you. It is not easy to get defeated, time after time, until you get better. It is not easy to open yourself up to hearing that you are not the best. You haven't arrived. You have more work to do. There is no replacement for having a teacher with a perspective you will never have.

One of the most common pieces of feedback I get from my students in defensive tactics training is this: it is really, really hard to get so close to other people for the first three months. It is uncomfortable and awkward. But now, those same people have a depth of confidence that they didn't even think was possible.

Getting close to others is awkward. It's tough. But it is absolutely worthwhile.

Being asked the tough questions on a regular basis by another person who is walking on the high road with you is one of the most beneficial things you will ever do. Just the other day, I was helping a wiser, older friend who was building a cabin. I was there at a time when I was going through a rough patch. I'm too darn stubborn to ask for help, but I needed to be refreshed. I needed encouragement and he knew it. So, he invited me out to help.

At the end of the day, he asked me, "Is there anything I haven't asked you that you were hoping I wouldn't?"

Holy cow. Fact is, there was.

I never would have faced the problem if he hadn't backed me into a corner and asked me. It allowed the Master to shed his vision in an area I wasn't letting him go.

We need teachers. We need senseis to teach us, correct us, and help us grow. We need brothers and sisters to hang onto as we walk along the perilous paths of the high road. And we need to hang onto them.

In the ancient days, the most powerful formation in battle was known as the shield wall. One man could not perform it on his own. Not even two, or three. It took a legion of men to do it correctly, interlocking their shields and spears together to form a phalanx formation. They combined their strengths by relying on each other.

When an enemy faced a shield wall, they weren't facing an army of individual men. Then were facing one giant unit, moving and working as a whole. The shield wall was unbeatable. Unless it was breached.

Alone you are vulnerable. Together you are impenetrable. When a person who loves me and sees the vision the Master has for me offers a sharp rebuke, it is not a time for me to throw up my defenses and develop excuses. The truth is, they see the enemy's spear heading for my head and are trying to push me out of the way.

When a follower of the vision is trying to save your life, let them.

When you see a follower of the vision in peril, go to their aid! Stand! Fight for what you believe!

For the followers of the Master's vision, the shield wall is the Church. It is a place where those who believe can come and stand side by side with others holding the same shield. It is a place for those who are seeking the truth to come answer questions and find a wholeness, together, with similar people walking a similar road, seeking the vision of the Master. It is a place that the enemy fears, and he should.

A key tactic of the enemy in the modern world has been to nullify the shield wall of the Church. The Church has changed, in many cases, from brothers and sisters standing side by side united in vision, to something else. A party. A task. An experience. A face in the crowd.

You know what happens when marital arts gyms reach a certain attendance level? They develop new trainers from within, and those trainers go start their own gyms, bringing a dedicated group of followers with them. When gyms don't do that, attendance soars and actual hand-to-hand training diminishes due to the change of environment. Then those meetings start getting called conferences.

If your vision is honed simply by attending a weekly, large group conference, you need something more.

Get into a shield wall.

Chapter Twelve

The Fires of Life

The Special Forces have a special saying: "when in doubt always look cool." I can see where they are coming from.

Maybe you are at a point in your life where you feel different... but you really don't look any different. Your habits are the same. You walk the same way. You hang out with the same folks as you used to. You treat others about the same way. But still... there is something different about you. You have begun to see things differently.

Something inside of you has changed. You've struggled to seek out the vision that the Master has for you, and you've finally begun to see the truth of your own identity. But the way you talk, the way you walk, and the way you carry yourself hasn't really changed.

Don't forget your initial vision. Don't trade in your vision for an easier road.

And don't wait for the fires of life to spur you into the next stage of development.

I can guarantee that you will find out one thing very quickly in the fires of life: the Master's timing is not your own timing. The fire is always a lot hotter than you expect. You didn't expect your girlfriend to leave you, or your spouse to have an affair with the neighbor. You didn't expect to get led astray so easily or enslaved by lust so quickly. You thought that bang was a water heater. But it wasn't. It was a gunshot.

And you never expect the heat to last as long as it does. You are stuck at your old, no-good job for years on end, just asking yourself what good you are doing there. You're looking for the path you're supposed to take to make a difference in the world. You're huddled in your room, the door barricaded. The seconds tick by and four hours later the police arrive to save you.

Abraham spent fifty years waiting to see the Master's promise to him come to fulfillment. Moses ran away from the Master's vision, fleeing into the desert where he spent forty years. Paul spent three years unseen after he got beat on the head by the Master on the road to Damascus. But their identity was not enslaved by a small, short-term master. Their vision was much bigger. So was their Master.

There is an ancient story that was written sometime in the early to mid-bronze age. It is, in fact, one of the earliest histories we have a record of, and it attests to a particular individual named Job. In this story, Job experiences a cycle of events that parallels the worst 3% kind of day we could imagine. In short, Job's entire life comes crashing down. He loses his wealth and his name, his family dies or is enslaved, and his body withers and falls apart. Job finds himself in the fire of life (which is ironic, because the Master thinks he is pretty good material) and he stays in the fire for a very, very long time.

It's a long read, so I'll tell you what happens: Job gets soft. His weaknesses and fears all come to the surface and spill out upon the ground as he gets hammered again and again. And then finally, when he is just at melting point, he meets the Master. Do you know what his Master tells him? The Master tells Job who he is and what his plan is for Job. The Master shares with Job some of the vision he has for Job's life and it is more beautiful than Job can imagine.

Brace yourself like a man. The Master has a vision for your

life.

It is about to get hot

When things get hot, they get soft. And when things get soft, they become moldable. You are the same way. Remember that the Master is using the fires of life to shape you and call you—and others—into a greater vision. But don't forget that there are other powers trying to melt you in that fire. Persevere. Remember the initial vision the Master gave you. Go back to his schematic outline of your vision. This is the most important part of becoming fully alive. Develop warrior roots so you may stand firm.

And when you find yourself in the flame, be careful what you surround yourself with. Trials and suffering can produce character if you seek out your Creator's vision in their midst, but they can also produce addictions and enslaving habits. Surround yourself with good models and set up your lifestyle for success.

If you ever find yourself stuck in a hard place, remember that those are the places where the greatest amount of growth takes place. Impurities will be driven out of you. Let that scale fall to the ground and let the pure heat refine you.

This is, without any doubt, why ancient followers of the Master say to rejoice in our sufferings: "for suffering produces perseverance, perseverance character, and character hope."

I have noticed something very interesting in the Book of Proverbs, an ancient wisdom text located in the Bible. It seems like whenever I read the word "love," the word "faithfulness" or "discipline" comes right before or right behind it. My takeaway is that you cannot have something as powerful as love unless you are willing to go the long haul. Faithfulness is not a one-week thing—it is a lifetime thing.

Those of you who are parents will identify here when the Master calls himself "Abba, Papa," in fondness and love to us. Remember that the Master cares a whole lot about you. It is central to the vision.

The truth of spiritual fitness boils down to your identity. Who are you? Remember, we are defined by whatever we've made master over our lives. When the last day of your life happens, you'll find out who that master is, for better or worse.

If the history of the world, modern research, and biblical truth are right, things are only going to get worse as time goes on. Trust me: seek out the truth NOW. We train at the gym so we can be strong when the time comes. We train so we can be fast and accurate when it is necessary to act. You need to seek out the truth regarding who you are and who you were made to be so that you can be confident. Get right with the real Master. Get right with your loved ones. Even if it takes sacrifice, even if you have to do all the work... that is why we put the time and energy into training: so we are ready.

Becoming fully alive will be the most beneficial thing you ever do, for yourself and for those around you. And to get there, you have to believe. You must believe that you were made for more than the mundane.

If you believe in the Master's vision for your life, returning home and back to normal after a traumatic event may not be that difficult. You may not feel guilt, or fear, or overwhelming emotion. Everyone will be asking if you are okay, expecting for you to not be. But you might be fine.

Not feeling guilt or fear after a critical, violent event does not mean that there is something wrong with you. Sure, sometimes a lack of feeling after an event can be numbness or disassociation. But it can also be because you know, without any doubt, the reality of the world. You just believe in the Master's vision to such a degree that it unnerves people.

I have to be very careful when a close friend or family member dies. Primarily, I am careful because, as much as I want to sympathize with the strong sadness and grief of others around me, I really don't understand why everyone is so distraught.

Yes, they are gone. But are they really? Everyone is sad because we'll miss them; and yes, it is true. But isn't that a little selfish? Is that really a good reason to mourn?

I talked about this with my wife, once. We lost a very, very dear friend named John. He was a man who walked with the Master. He counseled my wife and I when we were dating and was the pastor who married us. He died of cancer very suddenly.

There was much sadness. But I remember the last conversation I had with him before he died. He had only a few months to live and knew it.

"When I die, Greg," he said to me, leaning close over the table like he was sharing a secret, "you will be the one who greets me at the gates of heaven."

What? How can that be?

Sometimes it can be so hard to see the Master and his vision through our physical world. But doesn't the Master exist outside of time? Doesn't all of scripture and the words of Jesus paint a mind-boggling picture of time as being secondary to the Master's vision? Doesn't the Master say that, though we exist in time, time is not relevant? Modern physics agrees: time is a physical thing that can be slowed or sped up based on the interactions of mass.

All these ideas of purgatory, limbo, and the likeness of "the dead waiting around" are simply people trying to make sense of the Master's vision by fitting it into our own small picture of eternity. We try to do that a lot, and it never works. The Master's vision is so much greater than we can understand, or it wouldn't be a god-sized vision.

The thing about John was that he was so in tune with the Master's vision that it shaped his entire identity. Even in death. When he died, I wasn't upset. Not in the slightest. Because I know the Master. I know John. And I know myself.

My wife was upset. Very upset. And she mourned for John and the loved ones who were left without him, missing him. But

I wasn't. I explained to her why (she already knew why, but she is an amazing woman and let me fumble through it). She told me something remarkable that I will never forget. She said, "I like to think of my tears as love, love that I had saved inside of me to share with John. Now, at least in this world, I won't get the chance. So, they are coming out now."

Remarkable. But she wasn't done. "You knew John better than me," she said. "You knew him so well that you know he is still alive."

That is exactly right.

After a critical, violent, traumatic encounter, it is important to know that your response does not mean that there is anything wrong with you. If you weep, if you are scared, if you feel alone, it is okay. You are not alone, and those feelings do not mean you are a wimp or a coward.

If you are undaunted or don't feel overwhelming emotions, that doesn't dictate that there is a problem with you, either. It's always okay to check your compass and your heart to make sure you are in line with the Master's vision. But people process difficult realities differently. Love each other. Comfort those who mourn. Don't let anyone walk down that road on their own.

But know who you are. Know who the Master is. And take courage.

If you are already confident in your identity, then you can rest assured that you are always held in the hands of your maker. But confidence does not automatically dispel fear. Fear comes in all sorts of different shapes and sizes: terror, guilt, PTSD, depression, withdrawal... you name it, fear comes with it. It is one of the enemy's favorite tools because it drives a stake between our closest relationships.

In our culture, I hear a lot of prayers from individuals that focus primarily on safety. I hear prayers like, "Please keep my family safe, please keep my neighborhood safe, please bring my friends overseas home safely..." and so on and so forth. In the face of all the horrifying realities we are getting prepared for, I want to address this habit. Because I am not okay with it, and I think it is hindering our recovery.

Yes, the world is a dangerous place. We know that. We are ready for it. And we want the Master to intervene. This is a good desire. But one of the largest pre-cursers to trauma after an incident is not having expected it in the first place.

In many third-world countries, some of the values we naturally expect in the United States don't exist. For example, having a consistent roof over your head or a home to call your own is not always a guarantee in those places. And most of the time, the reason for the continual uprooting of these peoples has to do with what they believe about the Master's vision. Who knows if today is the day the government or the rebels will force them from their homes, and they will again have to move on to a new place?

I'm not downplaying how hard that event would be for anyone. But after talking to many refugees and foreign pastors and listening to their stories, what comes across is that they endured. In fact, they expected the trials. They expected hardship. They took it in stride. And it seems to me that very few suffered overwhelming trauma during recovery.

I want you to go back through our vision, the Bible, and count how many times the followers of the Master pray for safety. I'll spoil it for you: they *never* do. You will not find a single prayer from the apostles in the New Testament, or even in the old stories, regarding safety. Not one. What you do find are prayers for boldness. You find prayers for confidence and faith under fire. You find prayers for strength when facing death and daunting circumstances.

This is because those early followers of the Master understood that walking fully alive in his vision requires an element of danger. It is, by its very nature, unsafe.

When our material things get stolen or our physical treasures damaged, we often consider it a very traumatic event.

142

To take things to the next extreme, when our bodies get hurt and we are assaulted, those moments are naturally considered to be very traumatic experiences.

I understand why. Of course. What a loss. So much damage.

But what if we did not consider these material things to be our own? What if even our bodies were not our own, but just a temporary tool that we were entrusted with? What if all belonged to the Master, and we believed, beyond any doubt, that nothing could separate us from the Master's vision? How would that change our perspective? More importantly, how would that affect our recovery after a traumatic incident?

I want to challenge you to stop praying for safety. I want you to start praying for boldness. I want to challenge your expectations of security. I want you to be able to let it all go in an instant. I want your eyes to be set on the vision. I want you, like Job, to recognize that the Lord gives and the Lord takes away. All that we have is his; we are merely stewards and guardians. May the name of the Lord be praised.

To become one with the Master's vision, we are going to have to put to death our worldly expectations. This will not only sow the seeds of fullness in our daily lives, it will help us heal after the 3% day. Find rest. Find life in the Master.

The greatest casualty in any traumatic, violent event is a fracturing of relationships between us, the Master, and each other.

I always share a quote in my training classes. It is a line from Viktor Frankl, a survivor of four concentration camps. He says, "When we are no longer able to change a situation, we are challenged to change ourselves."

While true, and a great learning point for us all, Frankl's statement is just not enough. No matter how much we change, we can't do it on our own. We were designed to fight through difficult circumstances together.

I remember my first active shooter incident. I was just a

high-school kid walking to math period. As I walked through the courtyard between our cafeteria and main hall, I remember seeing Jo and his new girlfriend walking out through the doors ahead. I was about to walk through them when the shots started.

I immediately went into Code Black. I don't remember hearing the shots or seeing the crowd scatter. What I remember seeing is the face of Jo's girlfriend. She was about ten feet away from me, her mouth opened in a horrified scream as Jo fell. No noise. Then I remember being behind a garbage can—one of those concrete ones. I saw a teacher running the opposite direction as everyone else. He was running towards what I was running away from. Then I'm in the gym, a few hundred yards away. No memory, no idea how I got there.

I really don't know how that incident affected me, except that it did.

I am no counselor. I am not a healer or a doctor. But I can attest that the only place I have found healing, fullness, and renewal from personal trauma in my own life is in the hands of the Master, at the foot of the alter, and through open, transparent relationships.

The foundation of our conversation, this whole time, has been simple: the Master is with us and for us. There is nothing more powerful than laying down our burdens and our fears at the Master's feet. I think the Master can draw us to this place, to our knees, anywhere—in the mountains, at home, or in our shield wall. He longs for us to come back to him, to dwell in life, and to be in relationship with him.

Even though it is difficult, being raw and real with other people—especially the men and women in your shield wall—is a key strategy for remaining whole. These are your brothers and sisters, the sages and wise men that you have surrounded yourself with, who know and believe in the Master's vision. Be real with them. Let them in. Listen to their words of healing and guidance.

They won't be able to fix your problems or take away the pain. But they can draw you near the feet of the Master, even closer than you are now. He is the healer. He is the one that makes all things new. And one day, you will be able to lead others to the place of healing through your own story.

There is a reason why, at the end of Ephesians, Paul says to stand firm. He doesn't tell us to charge forward. Or to retreat.

He tells us to hold the line. Stand firm. Be one with the shield wall.

When you finish reading this book, I want you to be better prepared for the lethal-force encounter and *any* crisis moment in your life. Your tactics will matter. Your awareness will matter. But in the end, it will be your belief that defines what you do and who you are. Seek out that path. Dedicate yourself to walking with the Master. Then you will truly know what it means to live into your calling of full life, to be able to act in emergency events without fear or regret.

I look back and remember where I started: I was young, seeking my own vision. Alone, even when others were near me. Muffled by the mundane grind of life. Scared, when I really looked deep enough.

I never could have guessed where the Master's vision would take me. But this is how the Master has proven to work, time and time again. He exceeds our expectations and breaks open the definitions we have so casually set in stone.

The Master's vision calls us to redefine our realities. As a race, we so often set things in stone and then walk away from them. Tired of trying and failing, I suppose. I wonder, as I write to you, what swords I have placed in stone. What dreams I have cemented. What aspirations I have buried.

I'll tell you the truth about my life: the Master has been the hero of my story. He has allowed and provided me the strength to do everything that I once dreamed, though never in the way I imagined it working. He has held on to me when the seas were high and, to bring me home, has reminded me of his vision.

Every time I have trusted the Master, put my hand to the sword in the stone, and given a tug, it has come free. It is hanging on that is the trick! And I'm not talking about hanging on to the sword—I'm talking about hanging on to the vision.

From time to time, I find myself drawn to walk among our final stones: headstones. Walking among the graves of others hammers upon my heart the importance of praying for those left behind and remembering that I will someday lay among the silent, no matter how prepared I am.

I have long been amazed at what people say as their final sentence. Think about it: if you had two lines to summarize your entire life, two lines that would be all people remembered of you, what would they be? I've seen some pretty amazing headstones, but none as powerful as that of William Carey. He died in 1834. This is what he left as his final sentence:

"William Carey, a wretched poor and helpless worm. On Thy kind arms I fall."

William Carey translated parts of the Bible into over 25 languages. He was one of the most revolutionary missionaries and convincing speakers of his day. He founded colleges and established societies.

But without the power of the Master's vision, he knew he was nothing.

So be patient with the fire.

Trust the Master to forge you into his vision.

And boldly believe the truth, in any situation you find yourself in: you are a blood-bought, fire-tested heir of the Master.

On Thy kind arms I fall.

Appendix One

Glossary of Images

Credit must be given to Melissa Burns, who created all images specifically for this text. She has also entirely captivated my heart.

Appendix Two

Training Systems and Emergency Preparedness Steps

So, how do I start training? How do I get involved in being prepared for an emergency? I get asked these questions a lot by companies and individuals who want to be prepared but aren't sure where to start. There are so many options and so many variables. Assessments, training, policies, drills...

At the end of the day, preparedness for critical events starts with you. You must be able to face the fact that critical events might happen and CHOOSE to be prepared. Like any commitment, it is going to take time and money. You need to make sure you are focusing these resources in the right places.

Some of you may be thinking, "Why do I need this? Don't we have police officers and firefighters for just this reason? They do this stuff for me."

You would be right. They do. But unless you have enough money to pay an off-duty police officer or highly trained executive protection agent to be with you 24/7, chances are very high that they won't be around when you need them. In the average active shooter incident, police response normally takes between six and ten minutes. Six to ten minutes, while gunmen are actively killing individuals. Ask yourself this: how much can happen in six minutes during a gunfight? A major fire? An earthquake?

A lot.

Too much.

At the end of the day, preparedness starts with you. Because when the critical event happens, you'll be on your own.

This appendix will outline some steps you can consider for your place of work, your community, and yourself to help be prepared for an emergency event. "Appendix Three" will help your business or workplace start putting these steps into policy and procedure.

As we have already discussed throughout this book, everything starts with your identity: knowing and following the truth of the Master's vision, for you and for the world.

In addition, there are many other things you can do to get prepared.

What follows is a layout for readiness, but I want to emphasize that training can happen at any time. My team at the Tactical Training Academy loves training, because no matter how good your analysis was or how standardized your plan is, it is going to be YOU who has to act. I want to empower you to act correctly, even in the face of serious odds.

Business, Workplace, and Schools: Options for Emergency Preparedness

Safety Audits/Risk and Vulnerability Assessments of your facility.

In short, a risk and vulnerability assessment is a full security analysis of your facility. It measures your facility's vulnerabilities and calculates which risks (violent event, fire, disaster, etc.) are the most likely. This focus can allow your business, workplace, or school to spend time and resources on the risks that have a higher probability of occurring and the risks that are likely to be the most catastrophic.

A good assessment will include a full walkthrough of your site by multiple professional evaluators. When I do assessments, I always include climate surveys of employees, students, or tenants. They are the ones there every day, and it is likely that they will know something that the administration or senior executives do not.

A good assessment should also include an evaluation of current policies, training documents, reporting standards, technologies, and other site specifics. There are so many different variables to consider that a thorough risk assessment can take many days, depending on the size of the facility.

To limit the length, assessments can be hazard-specific (just for violent human acts, for example) or multi-hazard. Some assessments can be very specific, like an intruder assessment. Just how easy is it to get into your facility without anyone noticing? You'd be surprised.

I have conducted many intruder assessments in schools, hospitals, and on business campuses. The vast majority of the time, we end the assessment because no one notices the intruder wandering around in sensitive areas. If they *are* noticed, they are ignored. If they aren't ignored, a blatant quick lie like "Oh, I'm just looking for the bathroom" turns people away every time. Of course, this is exactly why we do these assessments. After an intruder assessment, you can bet that facility is keeping a closer eye out for us... and other, real intruders.

Every assessment (or safety audit) should include a site-specific Mitigation Analysis Report with recommended changes, options, tools, and other feedback.

But don't stop there. Threats of violence will still come, and, take it from me, there is only one way to win in an active killer event: prevent it from happening.

Create a threat assessment team to analyze pre-attack indicators and threats on a case-by-case basis, as they arise. Do this for threats from the public, from social media, from students, and from employees. Bring together stakeholders and get some training for your threat assessment team. If you can create a safety plan early, you might mitigate a world of hurt before things get out of control.

Creating site-specific Emergency Operating Procedures.

After a facility has an idea of the risks and vulnerabilities it faces, a plan needs to be created. This plan needs to involve internal and external stakeholders and needs to be written down. It must be focused on what to do before, during, and after a critical event.

We call this plan an Emergency Operating Procedure (EOP). As you can imagine, any document that tries to nail down exactly what needs to be done for all emergency events would be a huge document. And these are.

Creating a full-blown EOP for your company can literally take years, depending on how motivated your facility is to get it done. But it is absolutely vital, not just for actual response and mitigation of an incident, but for liability. The United States is a lawsuit-happy society, especially when people get hurt. In emergencies, people get hurt. Who do they and their families come after? The deep pockets.

Negligence is not a legal defense.

If you don't have a written, documented, practiced plan, your company is setting itself up nicely for a fat payout to a traumatized family or former employee. Fortunately, the next appendix in this book is an EOP tutorial to assist you on this road.

Again, writing an EOP should include very specific, best-practice national standards and it should be done by a professional. If this sounds daunting, start off with some site-specific standard operational procedures. These types of documents are similar in point and purpose, but smaller in scope. They are designed to be a training and resource tool for site-specific employees and can include emergency annexes, communication protocols, critical resource maps, and emergency policies.

They can be much more manageable and might be a good first step.

Conducting on-site drills and exercises.

How you practice is how you will act in real life. If you don't practice, you won't act. You'll freeze.

The whole point of a drill is to analyze the weaknesses in your plan and response protocols and to fix them through revisions. Do the hard work of making a plan, then start looking for drills and exercises to test it.

Sometimes your team might need a little motivation. A table-top exercise can really open the eyes of your administration to how ill-prepared they are for an emergency event.

Drills and exercises are vital for the continued process of making the plan better. They come in all sorts of shapes and sizes, from a table-top discussion between senior management to a full-sized drill that involves multiple agencies, like police, fire, local hospitals, and government agencies. Drills and exercises are so important that they are required by law for many institutions.

Training, training, training.

You never train enough. Really. The reality is, the amount of damage that occurs in a critical event hinges on the preparedness level of individual managers and co-workers.

Training gets people involved and (good training, at least) empowers its participants during any critical event. Taking more advanced training is always a good idea. There is always more preparedness and more awareness for us to develop within ourselves. Get training in active shooter response,

Emergency Management (disaster, fire, flooding), First Aid/CPR/AED, de-escalation and control tactics, situational awareness, communication and incident command, threat assessment, and hazards that are specific to your facility. Once you do that, start over and get refresher training. Everything we train for and practice is a perishable skill, needing to be honed.

A quick word here on multimedia or E-learning-based training. Sure, it has its benefits. But the ability to translate the learned material into action is NOT one of them. Online and video-based training may be cheap and it may be easy, but it is not the best. We like the easiest and cheapest road, but we cannot make that sacrifice here. It may cost lives.

For violent events and critical emergencies, be a leader and encourage hands-on training. It is the only way to go.

Obviously, many of these things require a professional to facilitate.

Obviously, these things are going to cost money, both in time and resources.

But how much is it worth to save the life of even one person by being ready?

The unfortunate nature of my job as an emergency preparedness professional is that my team typically gets called in *after* a major event happens. That is when companies start taking things seriously. We get called in to deliver a pep-talk and offer a brief look at what could have been done better.

Typically, it takes a close call or real-time event to wake people up to the 3% reality. Don't let that be you. Live Trained. Live True. Live Tactical.

Individual Emergency Preparedness

As an individual, there are many things we can be doing to get ready, as well.

Perhaps the most important is just being on the same page as those closest to you. Create a plan with your friends and family. What are you going to do if _ blank _ happens? Fill in the blank, create a plan, and keep your eyes up. Remember, condition yellow doesn't mean you are a ninja, it just means that you are aware and have a plan.

I really encourage this with young kids. Avoiding talking about these things will just increase the likelihood of trauma if an event happens. Tell your kids the reality of the world. Tell them that the Master has a good, beautiful vision for their lives, even in the midst of darkness. Instill in them the seeds of goodness, hope, and courage. Part of that is helping them create a plan and being aware.

They don't need to be scared. They need to be empowered.

I love kids. They automatically want to know the connection between the vision of the Master and the reality of what is happening around them.

"Son, make sure you never get into a car with a stranger you don't know. Keep a distance from them, but be friendly and kind."

"Why is that, daddy?"

"Well, son, it is because there are some people in the world who don't mind hurting others. But I love you, and I want to keep you safe from those people."

"Why are they like that, daddy?"

Most of the time it's because they themselves are hurting, deep in what remains of their heart. But the bandages they are putting on their wounds are only causing more festering. It's because we have an enemy in the world. It is because, quite naturally in this broken world, the light attracts parasites.

The Master has a plan of good, though we as a people have sowed much wrong. My son is a part of that plan for good. So are your kids, if you guide them into it.

Kids. They have such great questions. If only we asked questions like these more often.

Invest in yourself by asking questions and getting answers. Take classes. Get a group of friends together who are like-minded. If those people don't exist, go get some training. You'll find like-minded people in those sessions.

For physical, defensive, and awareness tactics, you'll have plenty of local, private options to choose from. Have fun and find an accredited trainer. Do some research and look them up. Don't take their word on their qualifications. Find someone without an ego and with a good heart, motivated by the Master's vision.

For emergency preparedness, most counties and states have emergency preparedness departments that host free classes. Give them a call. Even stop by your local police department or fire department. Go talk to them. Go out on a ride-along. Ask them how they prepare in their personal lives. Guaranteed, you will learn some new things about preparedness and situational awareness.

For those of you that are managers, executives, or business leaders, the next appendix of this book is for you. Applying this knowledge to your place of work is a difficult but vital strategy to empower your employees. Read on and bring life to your workplace.

Appendix Three

Model EOP Tutorial & Template

Provided in collaboration by the:

Tactical Training Academy

Master Instructor Cadre

Welcome to the EOP Safety Strategies Tutorial

You have a mission. Family members, team-mates, and clients depend on you. Yes, violent incidents are devastating individuals, organizations, and communities; but there are simple steps you and your team can take to evaluate and reduce risks, prevent attacks, mitigate damage, respond effectively, and recover from violent incidents.

You have a mission of service. Preparedness will help you survive and continue to meet needs in your family and community. Do not trust luck. Do not expect to make effective plans during a crisis. Prepare now!

This tutorial will guide your corporate team through the step-by-step process of recognizing risk[1] and preparing for safety and success in a violent world. Emergency preparedness policy development and implementation is as easy as eating a chocolate elephant: cut into small bites and eat one at a time, with coffee.

The model for thinking and the recommended steps in this tutorial represent current recommended practices as of 2018, and are drawn from the Department of Homeland Security, FEMA[2], law enforcement, educational institutions, and

---

[1] *Risk Assessments must be professional, accurate, and acted on. Training is effective when it rehearsed and put into practice. Safety Strategies and Standard Operating Procedure (SOP) work only when they are adhered to.*

[2] *The Federal Emergency Management Agency (FEMA), has developed the "Emergency Operations Plan" (EOP) model to help regions, states, counties, municipalities, businesses, and other organizations survive and thrive in spite of crisis events. This tutorial is complimentary in design and can be tailored for your place of work.. An EOP template is located at the end of this tutorial. NOTE: implementation of these practices should accompany professional training and risk assessments. The EOP is never complete, it must be adapted to developing cultural*

research by many government agencies, private organizations, and individuals in the Emergency Preparedness field. Note that this document focuses specifically on the violent event. Doctrines have changed since the "Shelter in Place" and "Cordon Off" violence responses of the 1980s. Education and policy development must continue as patterns of violence morph and spread, and new technologies and training equip civilians and law enforcement to prevent and respond to violence. Proper planning today matters, and plans must be kept up-to-date: remember that your emergency procedure is, or at least should be, a living document.

This tutorial is designed to help you prevent and prepare to survive a violent event, but it can be scaled and applied laterally to prevent or respond effectively to other hazards you and your community might face like wildfire, tsunami, power outage, infectious disease outbreak, or whatever else your risk assessment identifies[3]. Prepare for the most likely and damaging hazards first, and plan for others as time permits.

Leadership must prioritize safety. Teamwork is an essential element of preparedness. Everyone must recognize and embrace their role and adhere to pre-planned policies if even the best of plans are to work.

The TTA wants you, your family, and your team to fulfill your mission of serving others safely, and without fear. Proper planning, scheduled training, and regular drills (when done correctly!) reduce anxiety, increase the likelihood of effective response, and empower individuals to live and work with

---

and community trends, and legal and technological developments.

[3] A "Hazard Annex" is part of the EOP and prepares for a specific crisis. A "Functional Annex" deals with an overall response plan (like evacuation, communication, or reunification) that could be applied laterally for several different hazards and is beyond the scope of this tutorial.

confidence, increased safety, and enriched lives.[4] Use this document as a guide. As you need further assistance, reach out to our team at the TTA or your local emergency preparedness professionals.

Serving with you.

Steve Harris, Emergency Preparedness Instructor

---

[4] *Securing funding for Risk Assessments, Technologies, and Training is beyond the scope of this tutorial.*

Safety Strategies: Building the EOP

This page intentionally left blank

Action Elements to be included within every Emergency Operation Plan:

How do I develop an actionable plan to empower my staff and prevent dangers from happening in my workplace? Five actionable elements make up the "Prevention to Recovery" cycle. Incorporating each element into your "safety strategy" creates a manageable, wholistic approach to emergency preparedness. In the following pages, this tutorial will discuss each in detail.

1. Risk Assessment and Reduction

A professional risk assessment includes policy and document reviews, interviews and questionnaires for staff and students/clients/residents, and a physical assessment of the facility. The findings are combined with information about local environmental, community, and industrial hazards to **identify risks** and develop and implement strategies to **reduce them**.

2. Prevention

Targeted violence is premeditated and prepared for; reactive violence is a spontaneous expression of aggression. **Prevention strategies** for both kinds of attacks include Staff Training, Crime Prevention Through Environmental Design (CPTED), Community Presence and Involvement, and Technology.

3. Mitigation

Mitigation strategies aim to limit the havoc caused by an act of violence. Mitigation is dependent on CPTED, staff training, and is strengthened by communication and regular drills. The vast majority of catastrophic potential events never occur, or fail to have their maximum negative impact because of effective risk reduction, prevention, and mitigation.

(Consider a nuclear energy plant; radiation leaks are potentially catastrophic, and relatively rare due to prevention and mitigation strategies.)

4. Responding Effectively

Effective response strategies save lives! Ineffective response and panic often cost lives. Sometimes a violent event happens in spite of preventative measures. Objectively facing the risk of an attack prepares teams to develop and rehearse strategies for **response**. Regular training empowers effective response!

5. Recovery

"The grass comes up green." Effective **recovery** strategies begin before a violent event takes place. Personal development cultivates resilience in your team members and contributes to the survival of your organization. It is essential to pre-plan strategies that correctly and productively influence public perception, and to prepare your team to resume operation as part of personal and community healing.

Safety Strategies, Step 1: Develop a Leadership Team

Those who draft your safety plan[5] should be good communicators familiar with every aspect of your place of employment and the work therein. Teams will vary in size. Here is the roster of an imaginary EOP Drafting and Development Team we will use as an example in this tutorial. We will call them the "EOP Drafting Team".

EOP Drafting Team Member	Role in Workplace	Role on EOP Drafting Team
Billie Johnson	Executive Director	Chair
Eva Turner	System Administrator	Interviews and Recording
Steve Harris, Tactical Training Academy	External Advisor	Facilitator
Wade Garrett	External Advisor	Consultant

These same individuals may play a role within certain action elements of the EOP but should not be confused with the Incident Command System.[6] A professional EOP will often include formal terminology in its introduction, stating its compliance with NIMS[7], ICS, and other liability reducing practices. As our tutorial is primarily concerned with actionability, we have eliminated this formality.

---

[5] A safety plan is professionally referred to as an "EOP", Emergency Operation Plan

[6] ICS: In short, a clear response structure should be outlined within a chain of command system, with pre-determined roles during a critical emergency. Who talks to the media? Who assumes command? Who assumes command if your CEO is gone? Due to the nature of this tutorial, detailed information on the Incident Command system is minimal. Consult the Tactical Training Academy for more details, along with the incident command information located in Appendix 4 of this tutorial.

[7] National Incident Management System

Safety Strategies, Step 2:   CONDUCT A RISK ASSESSMENT

You might use an easel and several large pads of paper. The information you gather during this stage will be referenced continually. The people you are protecting can help; your team will organize and implement many ideas they share. Expect to receive good insight from your staff and community![8]

Your EOP Development Team should listen carefully at the information gathering stage; do not worry if the lists of risks are long; many strategies you develop to counter one risk will protect your team from other risks as well[9].

Risk Assessment

Risk assessment identifies potential threats, the likelihood of those threats, and potential victims. The EOP promotes peace and health in our community by implementing protection for all elements of your oversight: staff, residents, students, and visitors. Consider vulnerable groups like children, the elderly, disabled people, and those who cannot easily communicate in English.

Our EOP Drafting Team determined that the following groups in their workplace are at risk.

Sample At-Risk Groups

Member Staff	Stakeholders	Visitors
Office Staff	Employees	USPS, UPS, FedEx

---

[8] The examples in this tutorial were largely contributed by clients interviewed by the TTA. We thank the many experienced people who contributed to our research, some through tears. Your team might not face all these hazards and will likely face unique threats not mentioned here.

[9] Cyber-security is not the focus of this tutorial, but it must be taken into consideration. Your information must be protected yet be accessible in case your primary offices are destroyed or rendered unavailable.

Maintenance Crews	Residents	Delivery Personal
Inspectors	Children	Guests of residents
Outreach Staff	Elderly and disabled	Utility Staff
Collaborating Agencies' staff (ie: Human Services, Law Enforcement...)	Non-English-speaking	

Risk assessment begins with "in-house" interviews and an evaluation of current policies, procedures, and practices. Experienced staff can compile a list of risks and prioritize them. Interviews also invest your whole staff in the Safety Strategies EOP process; this builds morale and makes plan implementation and drills more effective. If some of the input you receive sounds expensive, write it down in your notes anyway: "better mousetraps" are made all the time, and the cost for technologies often goes down.

Our EOP Drafting Team identified these sample risks through interviews and brainstorming.

Sample Risks Identified from In-House Interviews

Staff	Risks Identified	Ideas and Input
Front Desk Staff	Enraged Parents/visitors/tenants, Frustrated Parents/visitors/tenants, Misunderstandings with Parents/visitors/tenants, Individuals under a restraining	View of the parking lot and approach to the front door, De-escalation training, Remote locking front door, Window laminate (to prevent breaking the window beside the front door), Cut a hole in the back

	order, violent intruder, intoxicated/mentally ill intruder, active killer attack, civil disturbance (riots), street violence, personal job loss, gang activity...	of the office and install another door...
Maintenance Crews	Fearful or hostile parents/visitors/tenants, crime-in-progress (ie: domestic violence/child abuse) drug or human trafficking in progress, rotting rats, dried out cats, needles, dangerous non-residents present in the unit, Nasty dogs...	Work uniforms clearly identifying 'maintenance', Teams of two, de-escalation / awareness / defensive tactics training, "Maintenance in Progress" door tags, HAZMAT/BIO-Hazard training...
Outreach Teams	The Mentally Ill, the Intoxicated, Street Crime and Gang Activity, Targeted Crime (robbery, kidnapping, rape, etc), Staff stress and fatigue	Teamwork/Collaboration, Training, Mentoring, Communication Systems, Self-defense Tools, Body Armor, Body Alarms

The second step of risk assessment is interviewing other "Stakeholders" and looking at the totality of community factors. These include first responders, law enforcement, tribal health authorities, and other collaborating agencies (like the

Department of Health and Human Services or its equivalent.) These interviews provide insight into the resources available to help in crisis, as well as the needs of vulnerable segments of your population.

Our EOP Drafting Team identified these risks by interviewing stakeholders.

Sample Risks Identified by Stakeholders

Stakeholder	*Risk Identified*	*Ideas and Input*
SRO Area Sergeant	High drug usage	Investigate detection technologies; Security or SRO presence on campus; clearly identify rules and enforce them; Training staff on recognition search/seizure practices
Public Housing Tenant	Neighbors fighting	Please move my babies & me to a safer place
Public Housing Tenant	That guy you kicked out is back	Management should be more firm around here
Fire Department	Your workplace is hard to get an engine into.	Establish a knox box and first responder access
Health and Human Services	Building numbers are confusing	Can we get a unit-map of your area?
St. Francis Soup Kitchen	We think some children in our community are hungry	Can you help us raise awareness of our services? Do any of your staff want to volunteer?
Tribal Health Authority	Tribe members and children	Please remember to involve our services

A Risk Assessment has a formal aspect which is beyond the scope of this tutorial. You should hire or secure an outside agency to perform a formal Risk Assessment. You might engage them to conduct your staff interviews also. The Risk Assessment Specialist should also conduct a walk-through and visit your workplace. Their findings, along with their interviews of Law Enforcement and reviews of crime patterns in your community, will result in a list of recognized vulnerabilities, many ideas on how to reduce risk, and strategies to prevent or mitigate attacks and hazards.

Sometimes a professional risk assessment is not in the budget. Do not stall waiting for funding! Do your own risk assessment so you can begin the EOP process![10] You should continually update and improve your EOP.

Other Hazards[11]

Our EOP Drafting Team identified two other primary hazards which need addressed.

---

[10] Engage Law Enforcement in your research. LE knows your community and is committed to its health. LE is eager to help with preemptive measures. Sometimes they can provide input regarding risk assessments. Usually they will agree to a walk-through of your facility. Take notes! Resist caricatures. Schedule ahead of time.

[11] As this tutorial is primarily concerned with violence, we will not here detail other hazards which might pose a significant risk to your resident population and staff. Remember, those sections require a prominent place in your EOP. For example, a loss of power during wintertime can be devastating to elderly populations and the disabled. Floods are often catastrophic to transient populations, and to communities of migrant workers. Consider all aspects of your community. Address the most likely and damaging hazards first.

Other Hazard	At-Risk Population	Risk Reduction, Prevention, Mitigation Ideas
Anhydrous Ammonia leak at "the Plant" *(an example)*	Public housing units in the potential plume drift	"Shelter-in-Place" training for residents, prepared statement to release through emergency alert system and social media, for each unit include emergency window and door sealing kits including door/window sealing plastic and tape. Simple am/fm battery or crank radios to use in case of emergency.
Tsunami Risk	Ten Section 8 units	Evacuation training, communication system

You should record the results of your Risk Assessment and interviews on large sheets of paper, or some other medium which is durable, readable, and easy to edit. List all your vulnerable groups. List the hazards and star the major ones which are the most likely and cause the most damage. List the applicable reduction, prevention, and mitigation ideas you received.[12]

---

[12] Professional Risk Assessments will outline risks, hazards, and solutions in a compact analysis summary document, taking into consideration specialty intruder assessments, crime mapping data, and other environmental factors not listed here.

Safety Strategies, Step 3: ARTICULATE HAZARDS

Now that you have information and a frame of reference, your team will determine which hazards to address first. You will respond to each major hazard by creating a specific "Hazard Annex" which goes in your EOP.

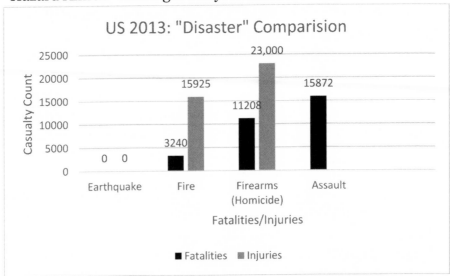

US 2013: "Disaster" Comparision

Ask yourself: with limited resources and funding, which hazards are the most likely? Which ones will cause the most damage? The above chart outlines 2013 data regarding just a few common hazards. Are you preparing for the right ones? [13]

Your staff, your residents, and your community will all benefit as you develop and implement effective plans.

Limiting the scope of each hazard annex in this EOP to just five things enables you to create a flexible, effective, actionable plan. For each hazard you address remember:

1. Risk Reduction
2. Prevention
3. Mitigation
4. Response
5. Recovery

---

[13] Note that "Assault" category injuries would not fit on this chart, at 1.4 million.

Our EOP Drafting Team determined, based on risk assessment, that their greatest threat was an attack on their workplace front office. We will look at the facts they considered and plans they adopted to create an **"Active Shooter/Active Killer Hazard Annex"** for the Front Office.[14]

To help get started on this annex, our EOP Drafting Team asked, "What are we are trying to prevent?"

The FBI and DHS define Active Shooter as: "An individual actively engaged in killing or attempting to kill people in a confined and populated area." But the Risk Assessment revealed that this was too narrow a definition for the threat. With many factors in mind[15], the EOP Drafting Team chose to abbreviate Active Shooter/Active Killer to "A.S." and use this definition:

Active Shooter/Active Killer: "Individual(s) targeting and actively engaged in killing or attempting to kill people." TTA 2018

The EOP Drafting Team also wrote a goal to help them keep oriented as they moved into creating a hazard annex for this risk:

"Our Active Shooter/Active Killer Hazard Annex increases the safety of Stakeholders at our front office."

---

[14] At the end of this tutorial in Appendix 1 is a pre-filled EOP Violent Intruder Hazard Annex for you to copy, modify and fill out with your own EOP Drafting Team for each of your offices, teams, and outreaches. (You can imagine how the safety concerns of an Outreach Team for Homeless Veterans or an Intervention Team for Teens differs from those of office staff, and will require a different/modified Hazard Annex in the EOP)

[15] A survey of active killer attacks reveals the use of vehicles, bludgeons, knives, plywood "shields", environmental weapons (like an I.V. stand and an ink pen), broken glass, explosives, construction tools, and other non-firearms are used in a lethal manner. Also, a violent incident with less than four deaths/injuries, gang involvement, domestic violence, or drug use is not always considered an "Active Shooter" event. We have concluded these are still catastrophic to the individuals and communities involved.

Building a Hazard Annex

This page intentionally left blank

Addressing the Annex, Element 1: Risk Reduction

Solving the escalating problems of your parents, visitors, tenants and staff is beyond the scope of any tutorial! Just remember: "winning" in a violent event is summarized through prevention. Safe communities matter and your mission can help peoples' lives!

How can we reduce the risk of an A.S. attack being launched against our community and staff? Considerations for Annex, Element 1:

I.   Institutionally understanding the escalation of violence enables workplaces to systematically implement de-escalation and protection strategies.[16]

II.   People who feel powerless sometimes become desperate.[17]

      o Disciplinary procedures might present options rather than endings and represent consequences rather than punishment.

          ▪ Consider how policies look to the people to whom they are applied.

              o Avoid cultivating desperation.

              o Consider restructuring policies.

          ▪ Cultivate a relationship with community intervention resources so you can refer troubled people.

---

[16] Consider training on De-escalation and Threat Assessment Teams (See Appendix 2 for a brief overview).

[17] Cultivating family and community health strengthens humans' natural "Violence Inhibitors" and greatly reduces individuals' capacity for violence. Many forces in the community strengthen inhibitors: individuals, families, churches, teams, tribal leaders, and civic groups are just a few. Corrosive trends which break down inhibitors also exist: family breakdown, drug use, domestic violence, gang activity, violence conditioning, the systematic devaluation of human life, and isolation are all growing problems.

- Implement policies of cooperation with groups and movements who build the community and reinforce violence inhibitors.
  - o Institutionally communicate and cooperate with Law Enforcement.

III.   Individually understand the escalation of violence and personally implement de-escalation strategies.

- o Staff who can recognize the Anxiety Stage of Non-Verbal Aggression and the Testing Stage of Verbal Aggression can usually employ practiced de-escalation strategies and reduce the likelihood of an attack.
  - Train the office staff.
    - o Research and schedule trainings.
- o Sometimes the escalation of an aggressive incident can be slowed long enough to bring in outside resources like mental health professionals, Law Enforcement, Tribal Elders, or on-site security personal.
  - Again, staff training and networking with community resources are essential.
  - Institute Safety Planning for at-risk individuals instead of "trigger" actions (terminations, evictions, etc.)[18]

IV.   Cultivate positive relationships in the community. Be available.

- o People demonstrate pre-attack indicators which are usually recognized by those near to them. It is important that your community believes you will listen if they warn you.
- o Cultivate a "We" culture rather than "Us vs Them".
  - Brainstorm with staff. Make plans, assign roles, schedule implementation and review.

---

[18] Consider training on De-escalation and Threat Assessment Teams.

V.   Take great care in the hiring process. Many problems were once paid employees, so do your research and selection carefully.

VI.   Cultivate personal development in the staff.

- o   Mission-driven and team-based.

- o   Research and implement effective, humble leadership models and accountability.

VII.   Evaluate vulnerabilities and reduce them.

- o   A.S. usually look for a "soft target" with a large number of vulnerable people. Usually the attack is rehearsed. The attacker often is familiar with the intended victims, and usually chooses a target with a high shock-value. However, if a potential target is perceived as being "hard", an attack is less likely. Here are ways to make your site "hard".

  - ▪   Attentive, trained staff
  - ▪   Controlled Entry
  - ▪   Visible Surveillance Systems
  - ▪   Security personal/police presence
  - ▪   Communication

Addressing the Annex, Element 2: Prevention

How can we prevent an A.S. attack being launched against our Workplace staff?

I. If an attack is imminent, contact Law Enforcement and implement your Move, Evade, Defend training! (More on this in "Response" and in section 3 of this appendix)

II. Activate your **Threat Assessment Team**[19]. When the Workplace receives a credible threat of targeted violence we will activate a Threat Assessment Team (T.A.T.) to evaluate the threat and recommend a response. The Threat Assessment Team is a powerful tool which, with practice, can be facilitated in-house (which speeds up the process and saves money). It is extremely difficult to prevent an attack in a public or densely populated area. **The Threat Assessment Team might be our most powerful tool for recognizing an attack before it is ready to be launched and for preventing it!**

   o Launching a Threat Assessment Team requires training.
   o COMMUNICATION IS ESSENTIAL FOR SAFETY AND CORDIANTED ACTION!

III. Respond proactively to threats
   o Utilize Community Resources
      ▪ Mental health
      ▪ Churches
      ▪ Tribal Networks
      ▪ Counseling, Family, and Addiction Services
      ▪ Law Enforcement.

---

[19] See section 2 of this appendix

Addressing the Annex, Element 3:   Mitigation

How can we mitigate an A.S. attack against our Workplace staff and lessen the damage?

I.   Crime Prevention Through Environmental Design (CPTED) is crucial.
  o Visible approach to entry doors.
  o Barriers to deny or impede access to intended victims like:
    ▪ Remote locking entry doors
    ▪ Shatter-proof laminate on doors and adjacent windows.
      o Train staff and fire department which windows will break for escape, and which will not. Laminate on every window can create a horrible trap!
    ▪ Locked or locking internal doors
  o Safe, easy evacuation of the whole building
    ▪ Exits should be clearly marked,
    ▪ Post evacuation routes
    ▪ Each area of the building should have two evacuation routes.
      o Chances are good you already have maintenance crews who have the tools and skills to install doors which improve evacuation routes.

II.   Training is essential to damage mitigation. Trained staff can accurately identify and respond to a developing crisis
      o Staff should be trained to recognize the escalation of aggression and pre-attack indicators, and empowered to act on the training.

  o Slowing the escalation of aggression gives other staff time to evacuate, gain reactionary gap, or barricade.

  o Evacuation should be rehearsed

III. Early detection and communication are vital; the sooner an attack is recognized, the sooner strategies to mitigate it can be activated

  o Visible approaches to unlocked doors.

  o Surveillance systems of parking lots and garages

  o Intercoms and alarms can alert the rest of the office of an attack, and also contact Law Enforcement *RAVE911 Alert Systems[20]

  o Weapon detection technology

IV. Policies

  o Restricted entry

  o Identification systems like name tags

  o Escort policies

  o "No bag, No bomb" rules about satchel, bags, and suspicious clothing or accoutrements.

V. Establish an Incident Command system for critical events

  o Know who is in charge, who is the back-up, and necessary roles that need to be filled quickly

  o Know who has keys, passwords, and can access critical infrastructure data (Rapid Responder Incident Command System is a recommended technology tool to assist with this process)

VI. Reunification, and accounting-for roll call

---

[20] This tutorial is not designed as an introduction to technology systems. They exist and should be used!

      o Decide on a virtual or geographic reunification site.

          ▪ Check in via phone, text, social media, email, or in person so each person is accounted for

              o Inform staff ahead of time about roll call policy

              o Record the presence of any guest, visitors, or parents/visitors/tenants who were present before or during the attack

The Mitigation element of our EOP Drafting Team's A.S. Hazard Annex looks like this.

Mitigation

Action	Acting WORKPLACE Staff	Directing WORKPLACE Staff
Bi-annual staff trainings in Move/Evade/Defend, awareness, & de-escalation	Everyone	Executive Director
Multi-year drills and exercises	Everyone plus Outside Agencies	Executive Director
Schedule and review CPTED upgrades	Building Admin.	Executive Director
Submit a plan of the EOP to local L.E. and review your plans with them.	Ex.D	
If anyone recognizes an attack **TAKE ACTION!**	Everyone	
If anyone recognizes an attack COMMUNICATE	Everyone	

If the attacker is outside, DENY ENTRY	Everyone	
If the attacker is inside, EVACUATE as a first response	Everyone	
If the attacker's location is unknown, EVADE/BARRICADE	Everyone	
When the event is resolved, contact your pre-assigned team to update your status & location	Everyone	Ex.D / H.R.
When the event is resolved, record the presence of any other guests, visitors, parents/visitors/tenants or others present before or during the attack	Everyone	Ex.D / H.R.

Addressing the Annex, Element 4:   Response

How should we respond to an A.S. attack against our Workplace staff?

"[The FBI's 2013 study demonstrates the need] ...for civilians to be engaged in discussions and training on decisions they would have to make in an active shooter situation." Special Agent Katherine Schweit, FBI Active Shooter Initiative

1. Prioritize planning and training.
   - Bad news: In a crisis people typically lose 60% function in their peripheral nervous system. Unless you have training, during a crisis you:
     - Panic, and panic literally is contagious
     - Cannot plan
     - Cannot hold a key to lock or unlock doors
     - Cannot unlatch a window
     - Experience mental dysfunction
     - Cannot load a gun
     - Cannot dial 911
   - More bad news:
     - Hiding under desks does not save lives
     - Waiting does not save lives
     - Compliance with the attacker does not save lives
     - Most A.S. violent events are over before the police can arrive. Many attacks are over before 911 is called. On average in the US, 65% of the time law enforcement response to an aggravated assault is between ten and sixty minutes.
   - GOOD NEWS
     - Pre-planned response strategies save lives!
     - Training/conditioning in Move/Evade/Defend is effective in saving lives!

      o   Trained responses are not dependent on the peripheral nervous system
  - o You can do the right thing without figuring out what it is
  - o You can do the right thing when physically or mentally hindered
- Trained responses can replace a person's need to think!
- Trained responses reduce panic
- Trained responses reduce lingering after-event trauma
- Trained responses empower potential victims to resolve violent incidents
- Stress inoculation reduces the potential for panic and increases p.n.s. function
- Training and preparedness reduce daily anxiety in children and adults
- One person responding correctly can help others respond correctly
  - o Panicking people often obey a trained leader

  o Training is available

  o Training can be a great personal and team-building exercise

  o Training reduces stress and increases performance in multiple areas.

  o Training empowers people (when done correctly)

2. Training and conditioning
   - Sharing facts, watching videos, and having discussions are useful, but will not prepare you and your staff to survive in a crisis
   - Interactive, scenario-based training and simulators have proven to be successful for

conditioning people to respond correctly during high-stress incidents.

- Stress Inoculation Training is a cognitive-behavioral approach providing people with added psychological resilience against the effects of stress through a program of managed successful exposure to stressful situations.
- Interactive scenarios provide valuable training, stress inoculation, personal empowerment, team building, policy testing opportunities, and many other benefits.

Watching online videos is not adequate training for an Active Shooter/Active Killer event!

Schools and many businesses have developed multiple, overlapping layers of fire protection and damage mitigation. Consequently, there have been few fire-related deaths or injuries at America's schools in the past 60 years! We hope the spread of Move/Evade/Defend and prevention-to-recovery strategies have an equally positive impact in the next 50 years.

3. Move/Evade/Defend: Your most effective response in an A.S. crisis:

- o **Move** is more than just running.
  - ▪ Recognize and communicate the attack
  - ▪ Move swiftly away from the primary threat (the attacker)
  - ▪ Recognize escape routes, cover, and concealment
    - o Avoid dead-ends, elevators, any place you might be cornered
    - o Recognize improvised escape routes like windows, vents, and ceiling tiles
  - ▪ Utilize cover and concealment

o Cover will stop a bullet, concealment blocks the attacker's view.

o You might run or crawl, move directly or tangentially away from the threat. Evaluate the treat and move accordingly

o Take others with you if they will come. If they will not, keep moving

o Keep moving until you are in a safe place, then call   911

o Give dispatch the location of the attack, the number of attackers, the number of potential victims, and the type of weapons, armor, or bombs involved

o **Evade** is more than hiding, it involves denying entry to an attacker, deceiving an attacker, or distancing victims from an attacker. Evasion is dynamic! It considers a developing situation! Stay prepared to transition into moving or defending!

In a hospital, kindergarten, or daycare setting, moving might not be an option!

If a threat is known to be present, but its location is unknown, evasion is your best option.

o Evade by effectively barricading
  ▪ Lock doors
  ▪ Securely block non-locking doors
  ▪ Turn off lights
  ▪ Move away from doors and windows
  ▪ Silence phones
  ▪ Keep silent and out of view until police arrive. The police identify themselves. You will see labels on police body armor; They usually wear visible badges, they might put

a business card under the door so you know it is really them.

- o Do not obey a command from an unrecognized source
- o Do not obey simply because you are called by name. Wait for a known source!
- Prepare to transition by Moving
  - o If you recognize that moving is safer than evading
  - o If the police or a known, trusted source command you to move
- Prepare to transition by defending
  - o If the attacker wields a knife or bludgeon, you might effectively evade with obstacles like counters, tables, chairs, or other environmental resources/weapons

Remember: While Evading, be prepared to Move or Defend as the situation develops.

- o **Defend** yourself and others!
  - You have a right to live!
  - You have an obligation to survive!
  - Surviving enables you to protect others!
  - Surviving is statistically possible!
    - o Twenty-one of 160 A.S. attacks studied by the FBI were resolved by unarmed civilians. Others were resolved by armed and trained civilians. You are not a victim!
  - Commit to your attack!
  - Utilize environmental weapons
    - o Tools
    - o Furniture
    - o Sports equipment

185

- o Any object you can wield to maximize force
  - Utilize teamwork
  - Neutralize a lethal attacker using any level of reasonable and necessary force
  - Move out of the area if possible
  - Identify the attacker to the police

Remember, you did not seek this interaction. The attacker's choices brought about this consequence.

4. When the police arrive to an A.S. site:
   - o Do not approach or touch the police
     - Responding officers will have weapons and be expecting to use them to save your life
     - Responding officers may not provide first aid or evacuate casualties until the attacker is neutralized.
     - The police may be wearing armor and helmets, or utilizing shields, or breaching equipment.
     - They may look scary, but they are there to rescue you.
   - o Obey commands to move, wait, lie down, or stand.
   - o Go where they send you
     - The police may be aware of secondary threats and are in contact with other first responders.
     - You can best help by complying
   - o Answer questions calmly
   - o Wait at the staging area you are sent to until you are released by L.E. This is essential to knowing who is safe, and to determining what happened.
   - o Make an accounting of who is present at the reunification site.

- Contact Human Resources, the Executive Director, and other staff via phone, email, or social media and let them know your status. This is a roll call and must be formalized.
- Record the presence of visitors, guests, parents/visitors/tenants, or others who were present before or during the attack.

The Response element of our EOP Drafting Team's A.S. Hazard Annex looks like this.

Response

Action	Acting WORKPLACE Staff	Directing WORKPLACE Staff
Recognize an attack and take appropriate action!	Everyone	
If the attacker is outside, DENY ENTRY (LOCKOUT)	Everyone	
Move! If the attacker is inside, EVACUATE	Everyone	
Evade! If the attacker's location is unknown, EVADE/BARRICADE	Everyone	
Defend! You can fight, win, and survive!	Everyone	
Evacuate to the reunification site	Everyone	
Do not approach or touch Law Enforcement	Everyone	
Obey L.E. commands and directions	Everyone	

Contact 911 if there is any question 911 has yet to be notified. Also contact a designated staff member (Roll Call)	Everyone	Ex.D, H.R. or 2nd in command

Addressing the Annex, Element 5:   Recovery

How should we recover from an A.S. attack against our office?

What happened? Who was impacted? What needs do they have? What resources do we have to meet those needs, and what resources do we need to procure?

These are real questions. Answering and responding correctly can be the difference between an institutional breakdown, or a recovery and continuity of services. It can be the difference between a painful memory, and a long-term personal breakdown.

Recovery is so important and can be so complex that it is typically written into its own section within the EOP, not inserted into each individual annex. This section can then be applied to multiple hazards, specifically any hazard that causes severe injury or a fatality. It is important for your HA to have a team detailed to put into practice steps toward recovery. This is true if the event is a single reactive assault on one maintenance worker, or a catastrophic targeted attack against an office of unarmed staff members.

Recovery requires **assessment** (both before and after an event) and **implementation** (again, this is before and after a violent event).

Plans must be made for recovery in these three areas:
1. Personal Recovery for Staff Members
2. Institutional Recovery/Continuity
3. Community Recovery and Healing

Personal recovery begins before a crisis does. Psychologist Dr. John Gardin II says that the elements which contribute to personal resiliency and the ability to recover after a crisis are many, but prominent among them is Spiritual Integrity. People with a clear and correct vision of their Purpose tend to respond better in crisis and recover better after trauma. Unforgiveness, disorientation, and unresolved issues all increase the potential for collapse during or after a crisis. Management cannot, in justice, control staff's personal lives, but Human Resources can identify and implement strategies to encourage personal health and development.

Training and preparation play a huge role in recovery – both by mitigating the damage of an attack, and by equipping people to view themselves as problem-solvers rather than as victims. This reduces feelings of inevitability and helplessness and cultivates the type of forward-looking attitude which is essential to healing.

Health services and follow-up are invaluable. Counselor Roger Horton once said, "Event is real, you have to walk all the way over the mountain..." Counseling and mental health services can be useful in helping individuals process the feelings related to a violent or traumatic event, separate those feelings from reality, and establish a new healthy, functional "normal". For staff who have sustained a debilitating injury, or who find returning to their old job impossible, it is important for your workplace to help them transition into a new position, or to make accommodations.

Institutional Recovery begins before a crisis does. Your investment in training and planning will make it more likely that your workplace will be able to continue its mission of service to the community, and again become a great place to work. Some parts of institutional recovery are reactive; other parts you can prepare in advance.

Community Recovery is a collaborative effort with families, groups, and community leaders. Grieving is a real and legitimate process. VIOLENCE IS COMMON, BUT IT IS NOT NORMAL. Healthy people do not initiate acts of violence. Crime and violence are abhorrent. Community response can be a powerful element of healing and can expose other potential threats in the community before they escalate into acts of violence.

Sometimes community recovery involves policy change in schools, churches, and municipalities. Be willing to engage in this dialog, your experiences and structure can greatly benefit others and speed their recovery and preparedness.

Our EOP Drafting Team asked and answered these pro-active questions:

- In case of an AS event at our front office, who will be impacted? What needs will they have as they recover and what can we do now to prepare to meet those needs? What resources do we need to procure to meet anticipated needs?

- In case of an AS event at our office, how will our institution be impacted? What can we do now to aid in our recovery and continuity? What resources do we need to procure to meet these anticipated needs so we can continue functioning?

- In case of an AS event at our front office, how will our community be impacted? What needs will our community have as they recover, and what can we do now to prepare to meet those needs? What resources do we need to procure to meet the community's need as they recover?

Our EOP Drafting Team relied upon the Incident Command System, deciding that the Executive Director would initially be in charge of recovery and would designate a Recovery Team to work in conjunction with the Public Information Officer. The Recovery Team would ask and answer the following questions, assign tasks, schedule follow up, and later meet with the EOP Drafting Team to give input on revision. (In many Workplaces, these teams will be made up of the same people in very similar roles.)

Our imaginary Recovery Team were to ask and answer these questions after a violent event:

- What happened?
- Who was impacted?
- What needs to they have?
- What resources do we have to meet those needs?
- What resources do we need to procure to meet those needs?

Complete, multi-faceted recovery includes immediate and long-term recovery. This is aided by a task force under the incident command structure, often called a *Crisis Response Team.*

An outline functional Crisis Response/Recovery element for our EOP Drafting Team looks like this:

Recovery/Continuity
Purpose of Section:[21]
After a major critical incident or hazard has occurred (particularly any fatality event) – what's our roadmap for a return to normal (how do we recover)?

- Immediate – Day Zero to Day Two
- Long-term – Day Three to Months or Years Later

Assumptions:

---

[21] *Instead of having a similar recovery outline in every annex, "recovery" is typically its own EOP section. This section is informed by best practices identified by the Federal Emergency Management Agency, US Department of Education, US Department of Justice - Office of Justice Programs, National Association for Continuing Education, and the American Counseling Association.*

- The ICS Team has been activated and appropriate action has been taken to secure the safety of parents/visitors/tenants and staff.
- An immediate response decision has already been made (Move, Evade, Defend; Evacuation; Shelter in Place; etc.)
- First-responders and Crisis Response Team have been activated.

Goals for Section:

1.   Return & restore the infrastructure of the company as soon as possible.

2.   Allow appropriate time and support for emotional recovery after a traumatic incident. (Recovery is not linear and individuals recover at their own pace. For some, recovery may take months or years.)

Outline

- District-level Crisis Response Team (CRT) comprises members from the Corporate Office, building teams, and community sectors like law enforcement, fire and mental health.
- Roles of District-level Crisis Response Team members:
  - **Crisis Team Chair**
  Convenes scheduled and emergency team meetings, oversees both broad and specific team functions, ensures that the required resources are available to each team member for assigned duties, and communicates with the building-level teams. The Crisis Response Team Chair is often an administrator or designee.
  - **Crisis Team Chair-elect**
  Assists the crisis team chair with all functions and substitutes for the chair in the chair's absence.
  - **Coordinator of Counseling**

Develops mechanisms for ongoing training of Crisis Team Members and other staff and identifies and establishes liaisons with community resources for staff and community counseling. At the time of a crisis, determines the extent of counseling services needed, mobilizes community resources, and oversees the mental health services provided. Must have appropriate counseling and mental health skills and experience.

o **Staff Notification Coordinator**

Establishes, coordinates, and initiates the telephone tree to contact the Crisis Response Team and ICS staff. Also establishes a plan to rapidly disseminate relevant information to all staff during regular hours.

o **Communication coordinator**

Conducts all direct in-house communications, screens incoming calls, and maintains a log of telephone calls related to the crisis event. Helps the staff notification coordinator develop a notification protocol for a crisis event.

o **Media coordinator**

Is, or works closely with, the PIO[22]. Contacts the media; prepares statements to disseminate to staff, parents/visitors/tenants and the community; and maintains ongoing contact with police, emergency services, hospital representatives, and the corporate office to keep information current. Handles all media requests for information and responds after coordinating a response with the media coordinator for the district-level team.

o **Crowd management**

In collaboration with local police and fire departments, develops and implements plans for

---

[22] Public Information Officer. Reference the ICS system.

crowd management and movement during crises, including any required evacuation plans and security measures. Crowd management plans must anticipate many scenarios, including the need to cordon off areas to preserve physical evidence or to manage increased vehicular and pedestrian traffic. Because of the possibility of actual threats to the physical safety of parents/visitors /tenants, crowd management plans must provide for safe and organized movement of parents/visitors /tenants in a way that minimizes the risk of harm to them under various threats, such as sniper fire.

- CRT will determine available business and neighborhood resources, needs and gaps.
- CRT will prepare staff to deal with the emotional impact of the crisis itself, and their role in responding to the crisis
- Visiting evacuation sites with staff;
- Requiring crisis drills.
- CRT will Prepare the community to deal with needs after a crisis. Providing informational pamphlets to families, staff and stakeholders about their role:
  - **Remain calm.**
  It is important to remain calm in the aftermath of a crisis. Families are greatly influenced by their community's sense of well-being, and anything that families can do to reassure involved parties will be helpful. At the same time, families need to be compassionate listeners.
  - **Attend to victim's reactions.**
  Be alert to emotional needs. Individuals recover from crisis at their own pace. Many victims will benefit from mental health services regardless of whether they were directly or indirectly involved in the incident.

○ **Return victims to normal routine as quickly as possible.**

Families should adhere to a normal schedule, and if the business remains open immediately after the aftermath of a crisis, it is important to continue providing a safe living space. Adhering to a typical routine will help victims in the recovery process.

○ **Refer Media to the PIO.**

Undoubtedly, the media will try to interview families and staff during or after a crisis. Staff/parents/visitors/tenants can make a very positive contribution by referring the media to the PIO.

○ **Attend community meetings.**

Families/parents/visitors/tenants will receive invaluable information and support by attending community meetings. Community meetings often provide information to help dispel rumors and establish mechanisms of communication with families, the media, and other affected parties.

• Assess the emotional needs of parents/visitors/tenants, staff and responders

• Roadmap for a caring and supportive environment

• Recruit community partners and volunteers to assist in a crisis (appropriate skills and certification) and plan for coordinating their support to meet district procedures and intervention goals. Impromptu volunteerism should be avoided minimize confusion.

○ Can we work with CERT trained community members through law enforcement?

○ Is CERT active in our area? (Checked w/ City)

• Return to business operations as quickly as possible

○ Plan ongoing interventions

○ May have to help families cope

• Keep the media informed

    o   Steps taken to attend to tenant/employee safety
    o   Services provided by the company
    o   Services provided in the community
    o   Messages should be translated
    o   Identify multiple means of communication in case of system overload or shutdown.
    o   Communicate with staff (No matter how well trained, a certain degree of chaos, panic or fear may impact staff.)

- Assess the emotional needs of staff, families and responders
    o   Who needs intervention from a counselor, psychologist, or other mental health professional?
    o   Identify recovery services for families or staff seeking treatment for victims or themselves
    o   Identify opportunities for appropriate group interventions for staff/parents/visitors/tenants not severely impacted by crisis.

- Equip employees and counselors to provide stress management upon a return to work.
    o   Caring, warm and trusting environment is critical following a crisis.
    o   Allow families to discuss what they felt and experienced.
    o   Encourage parents/visitors/tenants to engage in group discussions and address issues of guilt
    o   Consider: Group Crisis Intervention; Acute Traumatic Stress Management; Individual counseling;

- Conduct daily debriefing for staff, responders and others assisting in recovery
- Ensure those providing mental health services are supported with daily stress debriefing
    o   Debriefing helps staff to cope with their own feeling of vulnerability

- Remember anniversaries but minimize accidental glorification and sensationalizing of a perpetrator's actions (i.e. shooter or suicide victim). A memorial may or may not be appropriate depending on the incident.
  - Evaluation recovery efforts
    - o Which interventions worked and which didn't?
    - o Which assessment and referral strategies were most successful and why?
    - o Gaps in partners or strategies necessary for recovery.
    - o Need for additional training.
- Evaluate this plan with community partners, stakeholders and responders to determine how we'll interact in a crisis.

Incident Command System Team Members
- Members List (Business and Community Partners)
- Communications Team (Communications Team– Media, Social Media, Web updates)
- Death Notification Team (Law Enforcement)
- Points of Contact for family and victim support (Counselors, Police Officers)
- Integration with local, state and federal resources

Maintaining Procedure
- Law enforcement and medical examiner procedures must be followed, families should receive accurate information as soon as possible.

Ongoing or Evolving Emergency Communication when Reunification is not possible
- A plan for communicating when a tenant/employee is missing, injured, or killed, including how and when this information is provided to families, is critical.

• Planning team must determine how, when, and by whom loved ones will be informed if their loved one is missing or has been injured or killed.

• Communications when Reunification is not immediately possible (timely, accurate, and relevant information is paramount)

• Ensuring effective communication with those who have language barriers or need other accommodations, such as sign language interpreters for deaf family members.

• Non-incident response and procedures

Prevention

• Training of staff and voluntary training provided to stakeholders (community, parents/visitors/tenants). Make sure that your family has a plan in place and practices what to do in emergencies at home. This will translate into readiness at work. Being able to talk to them about the seriousness of emergencies and listening to whoever is in charge also plays a large role while organizing and practicing preparedness.

• Proper prevention and mitigation action can help prevent or reduce incident related losses. Detailed emergency planning, training of staff and other personnel, and conducting periodic emergency drills and exercises can improve readiness to deal with emergency situations.

• Establish/Confirm building crisis response teams

• Inventory staff with specific skills/training at each site. Consider First Aid, CPR/AED, Community Emergency Response Teams and/or Incident Command System training as appropriate for selected staff in each building.

ACT: An Example Emergency Preparedness Schedule

A key element of any EOP (and often the most lacking) is functionality. Policy must turn into action. An Emergency Preparedness Schedule, mandated by leadership, can help your team stay ahead of the curve and help turn your policy into action elements. This example schedule assumes an EOP is already in place.

DATE DUE	Annual Program Actions
	☒ Review Facility Emergency Operation Plan with Staff.
	☐ Update Incident Command Organization Chart with team roles and responsibilities.
	☐ Update Building Personnel Information– add new and delete old personnel.
	☐ Review Evacuation Plan (make sure they are posted properly in all rooms, kitchen, offices, and building exit doors), Building Emergency Response Map - ICS Team Stations & Staging Areas with Staff.
	☐ Ensure required Training is completed by Staff.
Monthly	☐ Conduct & evaluate Emergency Drills / and Input into documentation system
DATE DUE	*NEW* Program Competencies & Attainables
Monthly	☐ Site Safety meetings, including reviewing drill incident reports.
Monthly	☐ Incident Reports submitted for incidents

☐ Knowledge of Building & Company-Wide Emergency Communications Plan – located in District Emergency   Operation Plan

☐ Daily Two-Way Radio Use is understood by Staff.

☐ Daily ID Badge Use & Visitor Management Plan is reviewed by Staff.

☐ A Building Safety/Emergency Preparedness Team has been appointed to monitor Annual

Program Actions, Competencies & Attainables, address building-specific Safety/Emergency

Preparedness concerns; including conducting Emergency Supplies inventory.

☐ Building Emergency Supplies inventory and locations are reviewed and updated.

☐ **Staff have been certified in Move/Evade/Defend Curriculum, De-escalation, and Threat Assessment Team facilitation**

On-Going Trainings & Assistance

Trainings, Workshops, Drill Assistance, and Exercise facilitation is available and scheduled upon request.

- Evacuation
- Earthquake
- Shelter-in-Place
- Drills, Exercises, and Table-Tops
- Violent Intruder with Move, Evade, Defend
- Emergency Communications (Radios, All-Calls)

2017-18 Company-Wide Schedule (on flipside)

January   ☐ Updated Building Personnel & Emergency Contacts Information

☐ Updated Emergency Preparedness content for campus

☐ Update policy, new-hire procedures, and training plans

☐ Review Workplace Communications Plan with Staff (Emergency Operations Plan)

☐ Begin scheduling staff training for Move/Evade/Defend Violent Intruder certification program

February   ☐ 09/13 Emergency Radio Roll Call

☐ Update Incident Command System (ICS) Organization Chart for campus

☐ Create Campus Safety/Emergency Preparedness Team

☐ Review Emergency Procedures, Evacuation Routes & Emergency Supplies/AED locations

☐ Site Safety Meeting

☐ Company-Wide Emergency Drill: Evacuation Drill (Fire)

March   ☐ Schedule staff training for Threat Assessment Teams

☐ Review ICS Team Roles & Responsibilities, Team Stations and Staging Areas

☐ Review/Update Emergency Plans – (remove old outdated plans)

☐ Site Safety Meeting

☐ Company-Wide Emergency Drill: Earthquake Drill

April   ☐ Schedule staff training for De-Escalation

☐ Review Move/Evade/Defend Procedures w/Lockout and Lockdown

☐ Site Safety Meeting

☐ Company-Wide Emergency Drill: Violent Intruder

May ☐ Managers: conduct table-top exercise (environmental "cold weather")

☐ Review Reunification Plan *(indoor & outdoor reunification)*

☐ Site Safety Meeting

☐ Company-Wide Emergency Drill: Evacuation Drill (Fire)

June ☐ Review emergency plans with Fire/EMS/Law Enforcement

☐ Review Shelter-in-Place Procedures

☐ Site Safety Meeting

☐ Company-Wide Emergency Drill: Shelter-in-Place (Isolate inside environment)

July ☐ Managers: conduct table-top exercise (Hostile Termination)

☐ Review Lockout & Lockdown with Move/Evade/Defend Procedures

☐ Site Safety Meeting

☐ Company-Wide Emergency Drill: Lockout, Violent Intruder

August ☐ Update EOP from after action reports; Begin end of year data assessment

☐ Review Reunification Plan *(when offsite relocation is necessary)*

☐ Site Safety Meeting

☐ Company-Wide Emergency Drill: Evacuation Drill (Chemical Evacuation)

Appendix 1: Draft Violent Intruder Annex (TEMPLATE)

ACTIVE KILLER/VIOLENT INTRUDER

Resources

Communications   Fire/EMS
Transportation   Law Enforcement
Emergency Manager   Media
Facilities   Reunification Site
Executive Director
District Crisis Team
Human Resources

Immediate Response Action	Responsible
1. Call 911 Immediately. **Information to provide to 911 operators:** o Location of the active shooter. o Number of shooters. o Physical description of shooters. o Number and type of weapons shooter has. o Number of potential victims at location.	Staff
2. MED: Move & Evacuate, Evade and Barricade, or Defend Against Intruder.	Staff

3. Activate Incident in ICS Alert System. Once law enforcement arrives assign an employee to Unified Command. Corporate Office will be notified when the incident is activated.	Building Administrator/Office Staff/Safety Risk Management Officer/Executive Director
The first officers to arrive on scene will NOT stop to help the injured. • Expect rescue teams to follow initial officers. These rescue teams will treat and remove the injured. • Once you have reached a safe location, you will likely be held in that area by law enforcement until the situation is under control, and all witnesses have been identified and questioned. • Do not leave the area until law enforcement authorities have instructed you to do so.	
4. Notification to all corporate staff that incident has occurred.	Communications Director
5. Activate Tenant/Staff/Student Accountability Team. o Account for all Staff/Parents/visitors/tenants in attendance.	District Crisis Team/ Staff

6. Activate Tenant/Staff/Student Reunification Team. • Work with law enforcement. • Identified witness(es) – notify law enforcement	Staff/Law Enforcement
7. Activate District Crisis Team.	Executive Director
8. Community Notification – Unified Command	Executive Director/Communications Director
9. Complete if needed: o Employee Accident/Incident Report o Property/Vehicle Incident Report	Building Administrator

ACTIVE SHOOTER: PREVENTION & MITIGATION LOG	Date Completed	Reference
Bi-annual staff trainings in situational awareness and de-escalation		Attendance Lists
Multi-year drills and exercises		Annual Drill Log
Schedule and review CPTED upgrades		
Submit a plan of the EOP to local L.E. and review your plans with them.		

Threat Assessment Team Training and Activation→ Safety Plan Implementation		Confidential Folder
Communication Protocols reviewed and tested		
Continue to cultivate a positive, options-based relationship with all parents/visitors/tenants while maintaining clear healthy boundaries		Evaluation Log
Review and update hiring policies		
CPTED upgrades: Prune front bushes, remote front door lock, laminate on front door window and side windows, emergency exit door installed at the end of the south hall, pedestrian exit gates put in the back fence.		Facility Use Log
Regular staff training in public relations, personal boundaries, and Workplace policies		

Section 2: Threat Assessment Team (TAT) Training

The Threat Assessment Team process is set of assessment protocols and safety planning procedures overseen and administered by a unique collaborative team comprised of your local business, law enforcement, public mental health, and other local agency representatives. The primary goal of the TAT is to provide an immediate and systematic response to staff, parents, visitors, tenants, community members, or students who pose a serious threat to commit violence to others. Furthermore, the TAT also reduces over-reactive responses to Zero-Tolerance Policies that often result in a triggering event.

The TAT process is jointly a formalized process of investigating credible threats and creating an actionable safety plan long in advance of extreme violence. Both elements involve a multi-agency team, sharing liability during the development and implementation of the safety planning process.

Section 3: De-Escalation and Violent Intruder (Move, Evade, Defend) Training

No EOP is complete without functional hands-on training. When a violent intruder is in your vicinity, you must be prepared both mentally and physically to deal with the situation. The first and consistent WIN is prevention: Activate an early threat assessment team. Train your staff. Create a safe environment.

However, even with these important protocols in place, escalating violent circumstances will happen. Training on De-escalation techniques is key. Knowing when De-escalation must transition to immediate life-saving action is mandatory. Refer to the mitigation and response elements of this annex, or contact the Tactical Training Academy for more information on training your staff and stakeholders.

If you have further questions, comments, or a desire to partner with a professional team to assist with assessments, training, policy, or procedure implementation...

Contact your Emergency Preparedness Professionals:

Tactical Training Academy
www.Traning-Academy.org
info@Training-Academy.org